"If you're leading a team through nonstop change (and trying to keep people engaged without burning them out), The Unshakable Team *is the kind of book you'll underline, bookmark, and use. I appreciated the 'canoe' metaphor: when the water gets choppy, teams don't need more frantic paddling—they need steadiness, clarity, trust, and a shared rhythm. Within our team at PMS we often talk about this stormy season we find ourselves in."*

—Steven C. Hansen
PRESIDENT/CEO
Presbyterian Medical Services

"Heather Younger delivers a timely, practical guide for leaders navigating pressure and change. The Unshakable Team *shows how trust, care, and clarity build resilient teams that stay strong, connected, and perform when it matters most."*

—Marcel Schwantes
Executive Coach, International Speaker,
and author of *Humane Leadership.*

"Heather Younger delivers exactly what leaders need in today's high-pressure environment: a clear, practical path to building teams that don't just perform, but sustain excellence over time. The Unshakable Team *brings to life what I believe is at the core of leadership: when you create trust, clarity, and genuine care, you unlock ownership and resilience in your people. This book is a powerful guide for leaders who want to build cultures where teams stay strong, connected, and committed no matter the challenge."*

—Danny Langloss
City Manager, City of Dixon

"In The Unshakable Team, *Heather captures what it truly takes to lead through uncertainty—grounding yourself, building trust, and creating an environment where people can continue to perform at a high level. This book is especially relevant for leaders who are expected to deliver results while everything around them is moving."*

—Angel L. Cardoza Jr.
Vice President, System and Transmission Operations,
Con Edison

"This was the book that I didn't know I needed. Using a canoe analogy, Younger helps us gain insight and skills to manage wobbles; to become unshakable. She pushes back on the notion of 'soft' skills; recognizing that in today's headwinds of uncertainty—they are anything but."

—Wendy-Jo Toyama
MBA FASAE CAE (she/her) |
Chief Executive Officer,
AMERICAN EPILEPSY SOCIETY

"In The Unshakable Team, *Heather delivers exactly what leaders need today—clear, human-centered strategies to build trust, reduce burnout, and sustain performance. This book will challenge you, ground you, and ultimately make you a better leader."*

—Michael Bryant
County Manager, Mecklenburg
County Government

THE UNSHAKABLE TEAM

THE UNSHAKABLE TEAM

How Top Leaders Sustain Excellence When the Pressure Never Stops

HEATHER R. YOUNGER

WILEY

Published by John Wiley & Sons, Inc., Hoboken, New Jersey.

For general information on our other products and services or for technical support, please contact our Customer Care Department within the United States at (800) 762-2974, outside the United States at (317) 572-3993 or fax (317) 572-4002.

Wiley also publishes its books in a variety of electronic formats. Some content that appears in print may not be available in electronic formats. For more information about Wiley products, visit our website at www.wiley.com.

Library of Congress Cataloging-in-Publication Data:

Names: Younger, Heather R. author
Title: The unshakable team : how top leaders sustain excellence when the pressure never stops / Heather R. Younger, J.D., CSP.
Description: Hoboken, New Jersey : Wiley, [2027] | Includes index.
Identifiers: LCCN 2026025165 (print) | LCCN 2026025166 (ebook) | ISBN 9781394285273 cloth | ISBN 9781394285297 adobe pdf | ISBN 9781394285280 epub
Subjects: LCSH: Teams in the workplace | Leadership
Classification: LCC HD66 .Y684 2027 (print) | LCC HD66 (ebook)
LC record available at https://lccn.loc.gov/2026025165
LC ebook record available at https://lccn.loc.gov/2026025166

Cover Design: Wiley
Cover Images: AnnaFotyma/stock.adobe.com, Kyrylo/stock.adobe.com
Author Photo: Rebecca Bonner Photography
Printed and bound by CPI Group (UK) Ltd, Croydon, CR0 4YY

C9781394285273_030826

I dedicate this book to my children, who taught me what real leadership and teamwork looks like and to my husband, who happens to serve as the best teammate a woman can ask for as we jointly navigate the choppy waters of life.

Contents

Preface

Before we dive into the tools for building unshakable teams, I want to start with *you*. If you are carrying the weight of constant change, if your people feel stretched, and if you are trying to lead steadily and with care while the ground keeps shifting, this book was written for this season of leadership.

What you will read here stands on the shoulders of real conversations—with leaders and employees who were honest about what is working and what is not. It draws from the leader interviews I have hosted, first on my *Leadership with Heart* podcast and now through *Becoming Unshakable*. Additionally, my consulting firm commissioned the 2025 Employee Fanatix Team Culture Survey. Through this deep research, one pattern kept repeating: teams do not break because they lack talent. They break because pressure outpaces their capacity, and leaders are rarely given a clear system for steadiness and care.

I am not writing as an armchair observer. I have led teams through the disruption of mergers and acquisitions, the uncertainty of layoffs, unsettling reorganizations, and the strain of rapid technology change. I have seen how quickly morale can fray when communication is inconsistent, when workloads quietly grow, and when people feel invisible. I have also seen what happens when leaders choose steadiness and care: teams begin to trust each other again, execution improves, and people stop operating in survival mode.

This is a practical book. You will not find lofty ideals without a path to action. You will find clear behaviors, language you can use, and repeatable practices that help teams communicate under pressure, recover faster from setbacks, and stay connected to purpose and one another—even when timelines, priorities, and structures keep changing.

Right before the Introduction, you will find a page containing a QR code for you to scan. Once you scan it, it will take you to the Unshakable Team Stability Scan. Once completed, the scan results will help direct where you should focus in this book.

At the end of each chapter, I have a section callout that says, "Back to the Canoe," which is meant to re-center you on the main thing you can focus on from the chapter. Having said that, you will see that I provide plenty of decision matrices, key questions, and things to think about that will be helpful as you navigate the choppy waters of rapid change.

Then, at the end of the book, you will find a Steadiness Index. I invite you to use it to gauge how steady ***you*** are as a leader and then come back to it over time to track your improvement against that baseline. You might consider working through your results of the assessments with a coach or mentor to affirm the best route to take to ensure sustainable results.

This book is meant for people managers, team leaders, executive leaders, and those who coach and consult people leaders.

My invitation is simple: do not read this as theory. Read it as a leadership practice. Pick one behavior, apply it this week, and watch what changes. Then build from there. Steadiness and care are not perfection. They are choices you make again and again—and your team feels the difference.

Those who read this book will get **a simple, pressure-proof way to diagnose what's really happening on their team and steady it fast** using the strategies inside to pinpoint where the wobble is, choose the right behaviors, and apply practical tools they can use immediately (scripts, checklists, resets, and one-page maps) to sustain excellence without sacrificing trust, clarity, or the well-being of the people doing the work.

The more we get leadership right under pressure, the more our people can breathe again. They feel seen, supported, and capable—and they bring their best where it matters most. The result is not only stronger performance, but stronger people. If you are ready to lead with that kind of steadiness, strength, and care, let us begin.

Heather R. Younger, J.D., CSP
Denver, Colorado
May 22, 2026

The Unshakable Team Stability Scan

This book is not meant to be read like a typical leadership book where you highlight a few pages and move on.

It is meant to be used like a navigation guide.

Before you turn the next page, take the Unshakable Team Stability Scan. It is a quick diagnostic built on the five Zones in this book, and it will show you where your team is steady and where it is wobbling, so you know exactly where to focus first.

In less than 5 minutes, you will get:

A snapshot of your strongest and weakest Zones

A clear starting point for how to read this book based on your results

Practical next steps you can use right away

A simple way to track progress as you strengthen your team over time

This scan is free as part of the book experience because I want the work to be real, not theoretical.

Scan the QR code to begin.

Once you complete it, you will receive your results. If you choose to stay connected, I will also send follow-up tools and resources to help you build a team that can sustain excellence, even when the pressure never stops.

Introduction: Why an Unshakable Team Is Needed Now

Global engagement remains precarious. Gallup reports engagement hovering near one in five workers, with managers experiencing a notable decline, an important warning, given managers' outsized impact on team climate. Our own 2025 study echoes the strain: respondents cite excessive workload, role ambiguity, and thin recognition as top drivers of exhaustion, conditions that leaders can change (see Appendix A: Employee Fanatix 2025 Team Culture Survey).

The future of work is here, and it is faster, more digital, and more distributed. Microsoft's Work Trend Index describes a widening capacity gap: pressure to increase productivity even as most workers lack the time or energy to do their best work. Without new team operating norms, AI and digital collaboration can amplify noise, meetings, and context switching rather than relieve them (Microsoft, 2025).

Evidence is converging on what helps: clarity, flexibility, and psychological safety. APA's Work in America findings spotlight the importance of role clarity, supportive management, and flexible practices for well-being and performance (American Psychological Association, 2023). In Employee Fanatix's 2025 Team Culture Survey, flexibility and clear roles are the most requested fixes, and teams reporting trust and recognition show lower exhaustion.

In short, we don't just need better tools, we need better team systems. Teams require explicit decision rights, shared cadences, and recovery rhythms that keep humans, and human-AI teaming, sustainable. In this book, I set out to create a better team system that could be usable for leaders on day one.

How I Discovered the Importance of the Unshakable Team

The Canoe Moment

Some years ago, my family and I were on vacation in Key West. My husband, our four kids, and I had found this beautiful place to stay, and one of the free activities they offered was a canoe ride. My husband turned to our son—our adventurous, risk-loving 10-year-old child—and asked, "Want to go on a canoe ride?" Of course, he said yes. But the moment he settled into the canoe, he felt the wobble. The water wasn't rough, but it wasn't still either. He realized quickly that he had to rely on his dad to keep them balanced and moving forward. As they paddled out, the current nudged them further from shore, and he felt the unease of not being in full control.

"How was it?" I asked as they came back from the ride.

"Weird," he said. "I didn't like relying on Dad to steer. What if we weren't paddling the same way? The water kept pulling us out, and I felt like I couldn't control it."

"That feeling you're describing," I said, "is the essence of leadership."

He frowned. "I didn't like that."

"Most leaders don't at first," I told him. "They want certainty. But teams live with movement—currents, wind, surprises. The work is learning to trust the person in front of you, to call the stroke, to match the rhythm, and to keep balance together."

"So it's not about me paddling harder," he said, "it's about us paddling in sync."

"Exactly. Leaders fear the wobble—losing control, depending on others—but boats are built to be paddled by a team. When we share the stroke, we go straighter with less effort." He said, "I still didn't like that I couldn't just take control and steer us back here faster!"

In leadership, as in that canoe, the real challenge is letting go of the need to do it all alone. It's about building a team you can rely on, creating psychological safety, and embracing the shared rhythm that carries everyone forward. My son's "I didn't like that" is exactly what many leaders feel—but it's also the doorway to building an unshakeable team that can sustain excellence and thrive together.

How to Use This Book

If you are leading in a season where the pressure never stops, you do not need one more inspirational idea. You need a simple way to diagnose what is happening, name it in real time, and take action without burning people (and you) out in the process.

I am a system/framework-based thinker. If I can see a problem I and others have and create an easy way to think about it and align it with specific behaviors and strategies to solve for it whenever it appears, I already feel more grounded and less frantic. This way of being helps me remain more Unshakable.

The dictionary definition of "Unshakable" means *not possible to weaken or get rid of; not able to be shaken*. When that idea is applied to a team—people associated together in work or activity—it takes on a deeper meaning. Unshakable doesn't mean unbothered. It means **unbroken**.

For purpose of this book, then, **The Unshakable Team** isn't a group that never wobbles, it's a group that has built the habits and the systems to **stabilize fast**, stay aligned, and sustain excellence without sacrificing their humanity. By humanity, I mean the real human operating reality at work, people's nervous systems, emotions, stress responses, and limits. When teams ignore that reality, they may still perform for a while, but they become brittle, and it shows up as burnout, silence, conflict, and turnover.

Enter the Canoe Map and the five Zones that make it up. I use the canoe as the grounding metaphor in this book because it centers us in something easy to remember and in a real-lived story.

The Canoe Map

Think of your team like a canoe on moving water. In a canoe, you can feel the wobble quickly, and you learn to steady it fast, together. The five Zones described in this section are the main organizing principles for this book. Each zone has one or more chapters that help you name what is really happening, choose the simplest stabilizing step, and lead with care while still protecting excellence.

Zone 1: The Shoreline: Purpose and Priorities This is where you answer: Where are we going, and what matters most right now? Without a shared shoreline, good people paddle hard in different directions. You will also make sure to steady yourself enough to meet your team where they need you.

Zone 2: The Crew: Trust and Care This is the human side of performance: psychological safety, belonging, repair, and the everyday behaviors that help people feel seen, heard, and valued. When pressure rises, trust is what keeps a team from turning on each other. *Demonstrating trust through caring leadership*® in the right ways in the right moments means everything.

Zone 3: The Canoe: Systems and Structure This is your operating system: roles, standards, decision rights, and the rhythm of how work actually gets done. If the boat is unstable, even strong performers spend their energy trying not to tip.

Zone 4: The Signal: Communication and Connection This is how you paddle together: communication norms, feedback loops, handoffs, and the rituals that keep progress steady. Rhythm is what makes excellence sustainable.

Zone 5: The Water: Culture and Conditions This is the environment you are operating in: change, uncertainty, staffing constraints, competing demands, and the unspoken rules of the culture. You cannot control the water, but you can learn to read it and adapt without capsizing.

How the Zones Help You Lead Under Nonstop Pressure

Each Zone has three chapters, and each chapter gives you two things:

1. Behaviors to practice—the specific ways unshakable teams operate in that Zone.
2. A paddle—a simple tool you can use immediately (a script, a checklist, a reset, or a one-page map).

You will also see short callouts called *Back to the Canoe*. Those are the quick resets, the moment you pause and ask, Which Zone is wobbling right now? Then you grab the right paddle.

A Note on Caring Leadership

This book does not separate performance from people. Care is not the soft side of leadership; it is the stabilizing force that keeps excellence from turning into exhaustion. The goal is not just a high-performing team. The goal is a team that can keep performing, without losing itself.

What This Book Is (And Is Not)

This book is a practical guide for leaders who want excellence and sustainability despite what is happening in the water. This book is not about doing more; it is about building the team system that makes performance repeatable.

Who This Is For

Leaders of teams under constant pressure and living in uncertainty: healthcare, operations, customer-facing, regulated environments, leaders in change.

The Promise

By the end of this book, you will have:

- A clear operating system for sustaining excellence
- A set of repeatable team behaviors that reduce burnout risk
- A simple framework you can teach and reinforce to ensure that you and your team remain steady

Are you ready to launch your canoe? Read on to find a practical, zone-by-zone guide to help you diagnose where your team is wobbling, choose the right paddle for the conditions, and build the habits that make steadiness—and excellence—repeatable under real-world pressure.

THE UNSHAKABLE TEAM

ZONE 1

The Shoreline: Purpose, Priorities, and Steadying You, First

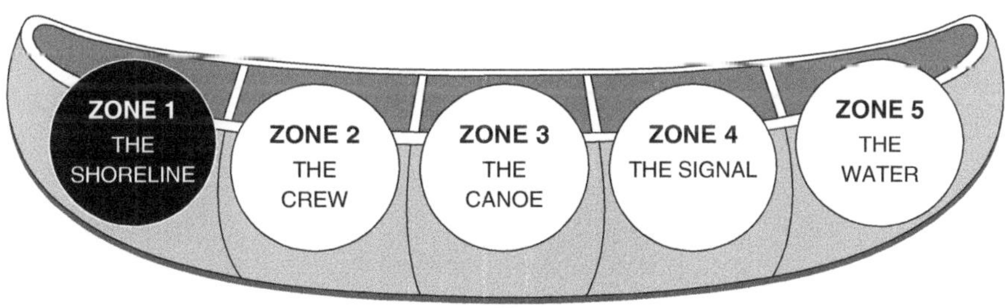

When pressure is high, teams do not need more activity; they need clarity. The shoreline is where you decide what you are aiming for, what "excellent" means here, and what matters most right now. You also make sure you do what is required to steady yourself before entering the canoe.

Chapter 1: Steady Yourself

Pressure is contagious, and so is calm. You will learn how to recognize your stress signals, interrupt reactive patterns, and return to a centered stance so you do not unintentionally create wobble for the team.

Chapter 2: Set the Shoreline

Unclear priorities create drag, rework, and anxiety. This chapter helps you translate purpose into focused priorities, tradeoffs, and a simple "this matters most" message your team can trust.

Chapter 3: Standards with Boundaries, Define Excellent Without Burnout

Many teams break not from lack of talent, but from unclear expectations and impossible loads. This chapter gives you language and practices to hold a high bar while building boundaries that protect energy, quality, and long-term performance.

CHAPTER 1

Steady Yourself

Teams become strong enough to handle what's next when leaders become the steady and caring foundation they can count on. So, before we talk about clarity and priorities, we start with the leader: how you enter the canoe when the pressure is high will make all the difference for your team.

Three Shoreline Problems with an Unsteady Leader

When a leader has not steadied themselves, three things happen immediately, and all three are Zone 1 problems.

First, the Shoreline gets fuzzy. An unsteady leader tends to speak in urgency, frustration, or overload, so priorities come out scattered. The team hears 10 things that matter, instead of one or two. That is how good people start paddling hard in different directions. I'll address this more in a bit.

Second, the Shoreline feels unsafe, not inspiring. If you enter the canoe reactive, your tone becomes the weather, people shift into protection mode, they stop asking questions, they stop flagging risks, they start guessing what you want. Alignment never sticks when people are bracing. I will address more of this when I talk about psychological safety.

Third, tradeoffs become inconsistent. Zone 1 is where you decide what "yes" looks like and what you will stop doing. When a leader is not grounded, those decisions change based on stress level, not strategy, and the team loses trust in the direction.

So, steadying yourself first is not a separate concept, it is the first Shoreline ritual. It is how you make your clarity believable, your priorities usable, and your tradeoffs consistent, so the team can actually face the same shoreline and move together.

Steady Yourself Before You Enter the Canoe

When the pressure never stops, leaders are tempted to jump in fast and start paddling harder. But teams do not take their cues from your intentions, they take their cues from your energy. If you enter the canoe rushed, reactive, or carrying your own unspoken overwhelm, the team feels it. And the boat wobbles before anyone even notices why.

When leaders walk into the canoe, they bring more than a plan, they bring a nervous system. There is real research behind this. It is called *emotional contagion*, the way emotions spread through a group through subtle cues like tone, pace, facial expression, and body language. In other words, people catch the emotional weather before they catch the message. Studies on emotional contagion in groups show that one person's mood can ripple across the team and shape how people coordinate, help, and perform, which is why leaders unintentionally become the loudest signal in the room (Barsade, Coutifaris, and Pillemer, 2018). That is why steadying yourself first is not a nice extra; it is a performance move. If you walk in activated, rushed, or carrying unspoken overwhelm, the team starts scanning, bracing, and filling in gaps. The wobble shows up fast, sometimes before you have even said a word. But when you pause long enough to regulate, even briefly, you give the team a different cue. You make stability louder right away, and you make it easier for people to think, collaborate, and stay in rhythm together.

I know this all too well. Some years ago, I was leading a team through what would be our second reorganization in less than six months, and I was overwhelmed by it all. After leaving a supposedly secret meeting, I realized everyone at work already knew what had been discussed. Well, I walked into my office, and my team could immediately feel that overwhelm. Most likely, they even felt my stress. Immediately after walking in, my team leader called me over to see how the meeting went. My gut told me to head straight to my office to decompress, but instead, I walked over to talk to my team. I told them more than they needed to know, and I immediately regretted not steadying myself first. You know why? I could see in their faces the overwhelm I had passed to them. I could feel their defeat in the face of my defeat. I realized in that moment how much my leadership impacted them, made them less confident and more shaken.

Looking back now, I realize that one interaction changed everything about my leadership. Going forward, I chose to be selectively vulnerable with my team, but I could not dump on them. I chose to do what I needed to do to calm my own nervous system so I would not have a negative impact on theirs. I learned that my taking even just 15 minutes to breathe deeply or walk in the sunshine after exiting a high-stress environment would put me in the best position to lead them well.

Steady does not mean emotionless. It means grounded. It means you can hold high standards and high care at the same time. It means you can name what is true without making people feel small or deflated.

Values Defined and Lived on the Water

In my book *The Art of Self-Leadership*, I touched lightly on the role of understanding our values in our ability to lead ourselves, and by extension, lead any team. I don't think I went far enough on that topic.

When I refer to values in the context of building and sustaining the unshakable team, I am referring to the thing we say we stand for as a leader. What can your team trust in your action and words? What can they expect from you to keep them grounded? Values are lived, not just spoken. How congruent we are with what we say we value and stand for is everything, especially when the waters get rough and the pressure is at its highest.

I want to challenge you to stop reading and physically write out on one side a sheet of paper an inventory of your top values. Some examples might be: Honesty, Excellence, Compassion, Family, etc. Then, I want you to take some time to write out the ways that your actions prove that you *actually* live them and even the ways that you do not. Be honest with yourself. You cannot build an unshakable team unless you, yourself, are unshakable. Naming your desired versus your lived values will be key to you understanding your blind spots. That honesty will inform how your team perceives and interacts with you, and whether or not they can return safely to the shoreline.

Based on my over 20 years of leading teams, the following list is a leadership check I developed that not only helps me get back into the pre-frontal cortex of my brain to think objectively but also steadies me before engaging my team in a high-pressure environment. Try this on for yourself if you find yourself where I was. This won't take very long to do, but you will save yourself the shock and shame you will feel if you don't take this pause before talking to your team.

The Leader Steady Check (60 seconds)

- What is the one sentence I want them to remember when they walk out of the room?
- What does the team most need from me in this moment—clarity, calm, courage, or care?
- What do I need to regulate before I speak—urgency, frustration, fear, disappointment?

- What story am I telling myself right now—and is it helping or harming the team?
- What is my most lived value in this moment?

Following that disaster of a story I just shared, this leader steady check helped me tremendously. I feel more in control of my emotions, and it forces me to pause before communicating an unintended message to my team. Of course, I adopted other practices like starting the day with movement and making sure to get sunshine as often as possible. By doing so, I steadied the canoe and readied it to receive my team when the moment arrived.

As I stated in the Introduction to this book, I wanted to create a paddle (some sort of helpful tool) for you in every chapter; a tool that helps you in a practical way when trying to be the steady and caring foundation for your team. This script gives you the actual words to use when the stakes are high and everyone knows it, and your team is looking to you to be the calm in middle of chaos of change.

Steadying yourself is the first move, but it is not the last. In Chapter 2, we turn outward and set the shoreline, so your team knows exactly what matters most, where you are headed, and how to stop wasting energy paddling in different directions.

Paddle: The Steady Entry Script

Here is a simple way to step into the canoe with your team when the pressure is high:

1. Name what is true: "Here is what we are facing."
2. Name what matters: "Here is what we are protecting—our people, our standards, and our mission."
3. Name the next step: "Here is what we are doing next, and who owns what."
4. Invite their voice: "Before we move, what am I missing?"

That last one, “invite their voice” has served as a grounding behavior during my entire leadership journey. It is a major difference-maker for creating an unshakable team. I will delve deeper into that topic in Zone 4. In the meantime, I want to direct your attention to setting the shoreline. To create The Unshakable Team, you must be in complete alignment.

Back to the Canoe

If the team feels scattered or tense before the work even starts, do not blame the team. Start here. A steadier leader creates a steadier launch.

CHAPTER

2

Set the Shoreline

In a canoe it does not matter if everyone has a perfect stroke if half the crew is pointed at the cove and the other half is staring at open water. The same is true at work. Teams waste the most energy not on doing the work but on doing different work at the same time. Alignment is choosing the shoreline together, then paddling with confidence even when personalities and styles vary.

North Star Values and North Star Norms

In Chapter 1, we talked about your values as the leader, the things you return to when the water gets choppy and your nervous system wants to sprint, shut down, or overcontrol. Values matter because they shape how you make decisions, how you treat people, and what you tolerate under pressure.

But here is the gap I see on a lot of teams. Leaders have values, the organization has values, but teams have not actually agreed to adopt and live a shared set of values together. So, when the pressure rises, everyone defaults to their own version of "how we do things," and that is when the canoe starts to wobble.

This is why I want you to build two things on your Shoreline:

- North Star values, the shared values your team is committing to live by, either your organization's values or a simplified version you adopt together, and
- North Star norms, the few clear behavioral agreements that translate those values into daily actions

Values Are the Why. Norms Are the How

North Star values are not personality preferences. They are the shared commitments that guide choices and tradeoffs when conditions shift. North Star norms are the behaviors that make those commitments believable and repeatable, especially under pressure. I use "North Star" partly because I am continuing the canoe metaphor, but mostly because I think that our values and the lived norms that make them real act like our compass, or our North Star, to get back to the shoreline.

If you are building an Unshakable Team, you need both. Because when values are vague and norms are absent, people fill in the blanks with assumptions, and assumptions create drag.

I learned this lesson the hard way. I once led my team through creating our own set of team values, five of them, and they weren't just a copy and paste of the organizational values. We built them together, people nodded, people felt proud, and it honestly seemed like we had real buy-in. But over time, I started noticing something that didn't sit right. The behaviors between team members weren't matching what we said we valued. The clearest moment came when I was made aware of a recorded call where two team members, not realizing it would ever be replayed, spoke badly about their team leader, someone they reported to. The team leader ensured I heard it, and I remember feeling that mix of disappointment and resolve, because we couldn't say we valued respect, professionalism, or teamwork and then let that kind of behavior slide. I pulled people in one-by-one and named what was unacceptable, specifically, and connected it back to the values we had agreed to. But here's what hit me after the fact: we had created the "why," but we never created the "how." We didn't codify team norms, the everyday rules of engagement that translate values into real-life behavior. And without those norms, people didn't have a shared, concrete definition of what it looked like to live the values when pressure hit or frustration rose. Ever since then, I've believed this deeply: values without norms are inspirational, but norms are what make them enforceable. Norms are what tell people what to accept, what to challenge, and how to hold each other accountable in a way that actually protects the culture you're trying to build.

What North Star Values and Norms Are, and What They Are Not

North Star values answer questions like these:

- What do we refuse to sacrifice, even when the pressure is high?
- What do we want to be known for as a team?
- What matters most when priorities collide?

North Star norms answer questions like these:

- When we disagree, how do we do it without damage?
- When something changes, what communication rhythm do we follow?
- When someone raises a concern, what do we do next?
- When we make a decision, what does ownership actually look like?
- When we are under pressure, what do we refuse to do to each other?

A quick distinction that matters:

- Values are often words, like integrity, excellence, dignity, service, trust.
- Norms are observable behaviors, like "We address issues directly, not sideways," or "We close the loop within a set time," or "We name tradeoffs when priorities change."

In canoe language, values are the Shoreline you are steering toward. Norms are the paddling agreements that keep the crew in rhythm.

Why This Matters More During Change

Change creates ambiguity. Ambiguity triggers fear. Fear makes people scan for safety. And when people cannot predict what leadership will do, they start protecting themselves.

That is why teams do not usually fall apart in calm water. They wobble when the water is loud and unclear.

North Star values and norms reduce wobble because they give your team something steady to hold onto. Even if people do not love the news, they can tolerate hard reality better when the way you lead stays consistent. Here are the steps to take to be sure your team is focused on their North Star.

Step 1: Align on Values Your Team Will Actually Live

Start by deciding whether you will adopt your organization's values or translate them into a simpler team level version.

Here is the simplest way to do it without making it feel like a poster exercise:

1. Put the organizational values in front of the team.
2. Ask two questions:
   - Which of these values do we want to be unmistakably true on this team?
   - Where do we drift away from these values under pressure?

Choose three to five values to adopt together as your team's North Star values.

Define each value in one plain language sentence, in your team's words.

Example:

- Integrity, "We tell the truth early, and we do what we say we will do."
- Dignity, "We protect the person while we solve the problem."

- Excellence, "We hold high standards, and we do not confuse overwork with performance."

The goal is not to invent new values. The goal is to agree on what you are willing to live, and make it visible.

Step 2: Translate Those Values into North Star Norms

This is where teams become unshakable, because values without behaviors are just intentions.

Use this prompt to turn values into norms: If this value is real on our team, what would we see people doing in meetings, in conflict, in decision making, and under pressure?

You are looking for repeat patterns, not one-off complaints. Most teams end up with norms that fall into a few buckets:

- Communication when things are uncertain
- Decision making and ownership
- Feedback and tension
- How we treat each other under stress
- Follow-through and closing the loop

You do not need 12 norms. You need four to six that cover your highest wobble areas.

Step 3: Codify Norms So They Are Clear and Usable

The test is simple: If someone new joined your team tomorrow, could they read your norms and know how to act?

Write each norm in this format:

- We do this behavior, because it protects this outcome.

Examples you can adapt:

- We speak directly to the person involved, because sideways conversations create stories and break trust.
- We name tradeoffs when priorities shift, because carrying two full loads creates burnout and resentment.

- We close the loop on questions and feedback, because silence creates anxiety and rumor fills the gap.
- We assume positive intent and still address impact, because care without clarity is not leadership.
- We disagree on ideas without attacking people, because we protect dignity while we protect results.

Notice how each one is behavioral, and each one explains why it matters. That why is what makes it stick.

Step 4: Create Buy-In Without Making It Feel Forced

Buy-in is not compliance. Buy-in is ownership of the outcome, and you do not get ownership by announcing norms like a policy memo.

Here is how to get real buy-in:

- Co-create the language, even if you lead the structure. People support what they help build.
- Ask for commitment out loud, "Can we agree these are the behaviors we want to be known for, especially under pressure?"
- Make it personal, "Which one norm will you strengthen first?"
- Make it visible. Use the norms as a shared reference in meetings, decisions, and handoffs.

Step 5: Hold the Team Accountable Without Becoming the Norm Police

Accountability is where norms either become real or become wall art. The goal is not punishment. The goal is steadiness. Use norms as shared language in the moment.

- "We said we address things directly. Let's take this to the person instead of discussing it here."
- "We said we name tradeoffs. If this is the new priority, what are we pausing?"
- "We said we close the loop. When will we update the team on what happens next?"

Build a quick norm check into your rhythm.
Once a month, ask:

- Which norm did we live well this month?
- Which norm did we violate, and what did it cost us?
- What is one adjustment we will make this month to stay steadier?

Use norms in one-on-ones:

- "Which norm feels easiest for you, and which one challenges you under pressure?"
- "Where do you feel the most wobble lately, and which norm would reduce it?"

Tie accountability to wobble, not character. When you correct behavior, make it about the wobble it creates, not the person's identity. "I'm naming this because I can feel the canoe wobbling. When we stop closing the loop, anxiety rises and work slows. Let's restore the rhythm."

Here is a simple paragraph you can use to introduce this to your team:

> *"I want to name something that will protect us when the water gets rough. These North Star values and norms are not rules to control you. They are agreements to steady us. We are adopting shared values so we can make decisions with consistency, and we are naming norms so we do not have to guess how we will communicate, how we will handle tension, and how we will treat each other when pressure rises. When we live these, we reduce wobble, reduce drag, and stay in rhythm. That is how we sustain excellence without burning people out."*

North Star values and norms are not something you create to make work feel nicer. You create them to make work clearer. When the water gets rough, they become the reference point that keeps normal differences from turning into personal friction. Values keep the "why" visible, norms make the "how" predictable, and together they remove a huge amount of guesswork that fuels unnecessary tension. Because once a team has a shared aim and a shared way of operating, you can stop labeling people as difficult or dramatic and start naming what is actually happening underneath: competing priorities, unclear roles, and misaligned assumptions about what matters most. And that is exactly where most so-called personality clashes begin.

Mission Clarity Versus Personality Clashes

Most conflict that looks personal is really about purpose and roles that were never made explicit. One person optimizes for speed, another for quality, a third for learning. None of them are wrong. Without a shared aim, these differences rub like gravel under the hull.

Often, I find this truth in my culture consulting work—specifically, when I am asked to conduct employee listening sessions to uncover what employees see as the biggest gaps to achieving a great culture that makes them want to engage at deeper levels in the work to be done. The team needs to know what each member is supposed to be doing and why they are doing it. When their roles are explicit and the why behind them is left vague, they go off course.

When the mission is clear, diverse styles become assets. The sprinter leads the first leg, the craftsperson checks the final mile, the learner captures what we will do better next time. Clarity makes room for difference. In my book, *The Art of Caring Leadership*, I spend a good bit of time going over the need to set clear expectations for the team. Think about it: How much more successful will the team feel if the vision is clear and how they are to meet it is even clearer? This level of clarity contributes to meaningful work. Team members stay and lock in to achieve greater things when they feel that work is contributing to a greater good.

In my firm's Team Culture Survey (EF25, n = 535), ambiguous roles ranked among the top contributors to burnout (25.4% selected this). On the solution side, over half of respondents (55.3%) pointed to alignment and clarity—clear roles/expectations or clearer communication as critical fixes (see the Appendix, Chart 2 and Chart 3; Table 1). When people do not know the shoreline, they paddle harder and still feel behind. When they know the aim and their part, effort turns into progress and frustration drops.

Something to note here is that empowerment without clarity leaves team members flailing. As the leader of this team, you need to ponder and plan for being crystal clear in what they are empowered to do. Once they know that, they will take calculated risks that achieve the vision and lead to higher levels of excellence. Otherwise, they might be afraid to step outside of the vague instruction you provided and stagnate your entire voyage.

Rituals That Reinforce Alignment

Alignment is not a kickoff event. It is a rhythm the team keeps together. To sustain the rhythm, establish rituals or habits that your team sticks to like clockwork to ensure you all stay in alignment in the work to get done and with one another.

The Apollo 13 mission is a powerful example of this because it shows what happens when the shoreline has to change, fast, and everyone still has to paddle in the same direction. In April 1970, an oxygen tank explosion turned a planned moon landing into a life-or-death return mission, and Mission Control in Houston had to rapidly redefine success, reset priorities, and keep hundreds of people aligned around one clear outcome: bring the crew home safely (Piccotti, 2025). What made that possible was not heroic improvisation alone, it was the Zone 1 ritual of continually restating the mission, clarifying what matters most right now, and making tradeoffs that matched the new reality, then translating that clarity into actionable direction for every console, every team, every decision. In other words, Apollo 13 is a reminder that under pressure, alignment is not a one-time announcement, it is a repeated practice, a leadership rhythm of naming the shoreline, protecting it, and realigning the team to it whenever conditions shift.

What Leaders Get Wrong Under Pressure

When pressure hits and it's unceasing, many leaders lose their grounding, which then makes everything foggy for those on the team. I think it's worthwhile looking a little deeper into what most leaders get wrong when the pressure hits.

Many leaders mistake urgency for clarity, and the team feels it as whiplash. Under pressure, leaders talk more, ping more, meet more, and change priorities more, but clarity goes down.

I remember leading a team of customer success managers in the middle of a merger of five companies and news of impending layoffs. The entire environment was distracted. Almost everyone on my team engaged in water cooler talk about who was being hired, who was being fired, what was happening with customers, and accounts. We were all holding on for dear life! During this time, the executive leaders were changing priorities faster than we could act on them, and they met behind closed doors nonstop. Yet, things got mirkier not clearer for any of us. Honestly, I worked hard to keep my team connected and as objective as possible while I also struggled with the "what if's" of the merger. The frenzy around the merger and the nontransparent communication made the shoreline fade out and the anxiety in the office increase.

Another thing leaders get terribly wrong when they are under pressure is **they try to stabilize the canoe with control, instead of steadiness**. Pressure triggers gripping, micromanaging, rescuing, and becoming the bottleneck. It looks like leadership, but it trains the team to wait, not paddle. A perfect example of this is the 2012 Los Angeles Lakers under coach Mike Brown, when the team attempted to install the Princeton offense (Jenkins, 2012).

In that early season stretch, the pressure to "get it right" quickly led to a more controlled, system heavy approach, and multiple reports described confusion and a slow start as the team tried to execute a new structure with little runway. In other words, the leader was trying to stabilize the boat by tightening control, but the unintended effect was that players started thinking instead of playing, waiting instead of paddling, and the team's speed became limited by how quickly everyone could interpret and comply with the system rather than owning decisions in real time. Again, control can look like leadership under pressure, but it often creates dependency and hesitation, which is the opposite of steadiness.

Another big and unspoken thing that leaders get wrong under pressure is **they think silence equals alignment**, and it costs them later. In pressure seasons, people nod, comply, or go quiet, and leaders interpret it as buy-in. But silence often means fear, confusion, or resignation. Think about my previous example of Mike Brown and The Lakers. The outside conversation at the time was that even with elite talent, the team looked unsure and out of sync, and the early results were messy because the system and the decisions were not fully shared in a way players could execute with confidence. When leaders assume a quiet room means the team is aligned, what they often get is delayed truth, it shows up later as missed timing, rework, frustration, and people waiting for the next instruction instead of paddling. I will dive deeper into this concept in Zone 5 when touching on psychological safety, but for now, the takeaway is simple, silence is not a green light, it is a signal to slow down, ask better questions, and make the shoreline unmistakably clear, so the canoe can move forward faster.

The Cost of Ambiguity

Recall the story in the Introduction of my son in the canoe—one thing was clear: his unease because he could not steer it back faster. When teams do not know the shoreline, they experience this same uncertainty, which leads them to any number of results.

Ambiguity Taxes Energy, and It Looks Like Busy Work The World Health Organization (WHO) frames burnout as chronic workplace stress not successfully managed, characterized by exhaustion, cynicism, and reduced efficacy (World Health Organization, 2019). In my firm's Team Culture Survey, found in the Appendix in the back of this book, 55.3% of respondents named alignment and clarity as the most critical fixes to burnout.

Here are some hard truths to swallow:

- Ambiguity creates anxious paddling, people work harder and still feel behind. This creates more stress, exhaustion and increases cynicism for the work that is in front of them.
- Ambiguity turns time into coordination cost, meetings expand, check-ins multiply, approvals get delayed and so does the work. This is a direct tie to exhaustion and reduced efficacy. At one point, do they just ask themselves, "what's the point of being here?"
- Ambiguity makes people feel like they are failing even when they are trying, because the target keeps moving or was never visible. This just creates more cynicism and stress.

Ambiguity Creates Friction, and Friction Turns into Conflict and Burnout Ambiguity does not just slow execution; it quietly creates friction between people. When purpose, priorities, roles, or standards are unclear, teammates start bumping into each other without meaning to. Work gets duplicated, ownership gets assumed, decisions get revisited, and little misunderstandings start stacking up. What looks like interpersonal tension is often a structural problem, nobody ever fully agreed on what mattered most, who owned what, or what excellent looked like. And once pressure enters the picture, that friction gets louder. People begin to protect themselves. They overexplain. They wait for direction. They stay quiet in meetings, then vent in side conversations. Not because they are difficult, but because ambiguity creates uncertainty, and uncertainty makes people feel unsafe.

Then the truth comes out later, in missed deadlines, slow handoffs, and people paddling out of sync. That is why I believe that clarity is not control, clarity is care. When you give people clarity, you give them confidence. You give them a way to make decisions without waiting on you. You give them the ability to paddle with strength instead of anxiety.

This showed up in the study result I mentioned earlier where 55% of respondents pointed to alignment and clarity as the most critical fixes (see the Appendix). That tells us something important, people are not asking leaders to motivate them more, they are asking leaders to make the shoreline unmistakable, then protect it long enough for the team to execute.

I remember working with a project team whose main responsibility was customer order fulfillment and service. At one meeting, I shared with the group about a customer complaint, and what the customer expected us to do to solve it. Then, a couple in the group were supposed to meet to come up with the plan and then present it the following week. I was unable to attend this presentation meeting, and in my absence, many at the table were making assumptions about why the customer wanted a certain solution. A couple of the project team members erupted into an argument about it. They did not agree on the final solutions. After I heard about all the discussions and assumptions in that room, I realized that the team's disagreement wasn't personal at all; they were just confused. Somehow, they thought the customer wanted a new order, but they just wanted certain parts of the order re-sent and a refund for the headache. Once I named what was actually happening (the *shoreline* we needed to get to), clarified who needed to do what and invited their feedback and clarifying questions, everyone was aligned on next steps. I realized after all the back-and-forth that they were feeling what my son felt on that canoe. They were uneasy about relying on others when they were not very clear on who was steering.

Paddle: Monday Stand-Up Check

Start-of-week shoreline check. Begin Mondays with a brief note or stand-up that answers three questions:

- What is the shoreline for this week?
- Who owns which stretch?
- What cannot move?

This takes minutes and prevents days of drift. It also increases the likelihood that your team will be more focused on the work to be done.

Once the shoreline is clear, the next question is just as important: What does excellent look like here, and how do you hold that standard without exhausting your people? In Chapter 3, we will define the difference between excellence and perfection, set boundaries around the bar, and show you how to protect performance without creating burnout.

Back to the Canoe

If all else fails, make sure you and your team can answer who, when, where, and what at any point in time.

CHAPTER

3

Standards with Boundaries, Define Excellent Without Burnout

In Chapter 2, we talked about why alignment matters, the importance of North Star values and norms and how ambiguity drains teams. Now, we take the next step. Once the shoreline is clear, leaders still have to answer a harder question: What does excellent look like here, and how do we protect it without burning people out in the process? Because when standards are unclear, unrealistic, or constantly shifting, even the most committed people start living in "never enough." That is when stress, exhaustion, cynicism, and reduced effectiveness begin to show up in the day-to-day.

One of the biggest barriers to holding boundaries around excellence is this: leaders and teams confuse excellence with perfection. And that confusion quietly drives performance into the ground.

Excellence Versus Perfection, the Distinction That Protects Performance

Excellence and perfection sound similar, but they produce completely different cultures. Excellence is defined as superior, eminently good, "first class." Perfection is defined as a condition, state, or quality of being free, or as free as possible, from all flaws or defects. I don't want to get lawyerly here, but I want to provide some clarity around what makes these concepts different using just these definitions, and then I would like to lean into the practicality of what makes them distinct.

First, let's look at these definitions a little closer. Excellence says nothing about any mistakes, flaws, or imperfections a person or a team might have on the way to achieving excellence. Taking this thinking one step further, being free of flaws or defects does not guarantee excellent outcomes. The canoe itself is a perfect example of this: most canoes are built from practical materials—fiberglass, Kevlar, aluminum, wood—none of them are perfect, and all of them show wear. Yet in competition, what wins is not a spotless canoe, it is a canoe with integrity, a crew with trust, and a rhythm that holds under pressure. That is the lesson for leaders. Excellence is not a "cosmetic" standard, it is an integrity standard. It is the ability to perform with care, even with a few scuffs, even after a wobble, because you know how to steady, adjust, and keep paddling together. Below are some powerful ways to see the difference between excellence and perfection:

- **Excellence is outcome-based and values-aligned.**

  It asks, what does great look like for the purpose, in this season, with the people and resources we *actually* have.

- **Perfection is fear-based and approval seeking.**

  It asks, how do I avoid criticism, how do I avoid being blamed, how do I make sure no one can poke holes in this.

- **Excellence invites learning.**

  It builds in learning loops, feedback, iteration, and honest debriefs.

- **Perfection hides.**

  It leads to over polishing, delaying, avoiding transparency, and quietly reworking things in isolation.

How do excellence and perfect show up at work? Perfection usually shows up as fear disguised as effort, it is the extra deck, the extra round, the extra late night, the reluctance to ship, the resistance to feedback, and the feeling that nothing is ever quite enough. Excellence shows up as clarity and consistency, the team knows the bar, knows the purpose, knows the tradeoffs, and knows what "done" looks like.

Even teams we all admire do not win because they avoid flaws, they win because they are clear on the purpose, they define "excellent" for the moment, and they do not waste strokes trying to make it bulletproof before it is useful. The company, Dropbox, is a perfect example of this in the wild.

Before Dropbox had a fully built product, the founder created a short demo video that showed the experience as it was meant to work and targeted it to the right early audience (Ries, 2011). The goal was not polish for polish's sake, it was clarity: "Do people want this enough to raise their hand?" and "What exactly are they responding to?" The result was immediate learning and momentum, their beta waiting list jumped dramatically, and the team could stop guessing, stop overbuilding, and start building what mattered. This is the excellence move under pressure—define "done" as "done enough to validate and learn," instead of "done when no one can criticize it." That shift restores speed, raises trust, and lowers the anxious energy that comes from trying to bulletproof everything in private.

I know this approach personally. I think I was meant to be an engineer in another life. I am a master at iteration and just trying and failing and trying and failing. Sometimes, I throw too many things at the wall to see if they stick, but usually this thinking drives up the agility of my, now, small team. While I believe strongly in excellence and putting my best foot forward, I never let perfection get in the way of the forward movement. My team knows this and doesn't over fuss before presenting something to me. They know I am open to seeing ideas early on and seeing what happens as we release and then tweak. While my company is no Dropbox, I choose to employ their same thinking, and that helps me and my team feel stable even with a little wobble in the mix.

In a recent episode of my Becoming Unshakable podcast (Younger, 2026), I sat down with Amy Edmondson. Amy is a Harvard Business School professor and a world-renowned voice on psychological safety, and her work has shaped how leaders understand learning, risk, and performance. In her book, *The Right Kind of Wrong*, she makes a distinction that I wish every leadership team would stop and absorb: if you want excellence, you cannot treat all failure the same. Because when leaders lump every misstep into one bucket, teams do what humans always do when we are trying to stay safe. They hide. They polish in private. They delay. They stop telling the truth early, and before you know it, perfection becomes the strategy, not because people love it, but because they are trying to avoid consequences.

Amy breaks failure down in a way that immediately makes leadership more practical. She describes three kinds of failure and what each one requires from us.

First, there are basic failures. These are the preventable ones. The kinds that happen when people skip steps, ignore a process, or do not follow what is already known and proven. Basic failures are not about learning. They are about discipline, attention, and consistency. They are the kind of failure you reduce with clear standards, training, checklists, and follow-through. In canoe terms, basic failures are when we already agreed on the strokes, but someone decides to freestyle anyway.

Second, there are complex failures. These happen in systems that are complicated, interdependent, fast moving, or under strain. No single person caused it. It is the result of multiple variables stacking up. A small miss, a handoff that was unclear, a tight timeline, a change in direction, a new tool, a missing piece of context. Complex failures are not solved by blame, because blame oversimplifies what is actually happening. Complex failures are solved by getting curious, mapping what happened, and strengthening the system so the same pattern does not repeat. In canoe terms, complex failures are what happens when the water shifts, the crew loses rhythm, and the canoe starts drifting, not because someone is bad, but because the conditions changed and the system did not adapt fast enough.

Third, and the most interesting kind of failure there is, is intelligent failure, what Amy calls "the right kind of wrong." This is the one most leaders say they want, but accidentally punish. Intelligent failure happens when you are doing something new, uncertain, or innovative, and you are learning your way forward. The key word is intelligent. These failures are planned, contained, and used to generate learning. They are the small experiments that prevent bigger, more expensive mistakes later. Intelligent failure is what you expect when you are exploring new territory. And if you do not allow it, you do not get innovation, you get fear-based compliance. Or worse, you get fake certainty.

Now here is why this fits directly into excellence versus perfection.

Perfection treats all failure like a threat. It says, do not get it wrong. Do not be the one who causes the problem. Do not give anyone a reason to question you. So, people overdocument, overexplain, over-polish, and delay shipping anything until it feels bulletproof. While that might look like high standards, what it usually produces is slow learning, hidden risk, and a team that is exhausted from trying to be flawless.

Excellence is different. Excellence says, we are going to be clear about what must not fail, we are going to learn fast where learning is required, and we are going to respond to mistakes with the right response for the right kind of failure. It keeps standards high without turning the work environment into a fear environment.

Here are a few simple leader questions you can use to keep your standards high without sliding into perfection. They are not scientific, but more intuitive.

If this is a basic failure, ask:

- What was the standard or process we were supposed to follow?
- What got in the way of following it?
- What do we need to clarify, train, or reinforce so this becomes easier to do right next time?

If this is a complex failure, ask:

- What conditions were present that made this more likely?
- Where did the system break down—handoffs, decision rights, communication, resourcing?
- What is the one system adjustment that reduces drag and reduces the odds of this happening again?

If this is an intelligent failure, ask:

- What did we learn that we could not have learned without trying?
- What did this reveal about the customer, the process, the tool, or the assumptions?
- How do we capture the learning and run the next small test with more clarity?

This is one of the most stabilizing leadership moves you can make. It tells people, we are not going to punish learning, but we are also not going to normalize sloppiness. We will protect excellence by being honest about what kind of miss this was and responding with discipline, curiosity, or experimentation, depending on what the moment requires. In canoe terms, it is how you keep the wobble from becoming a spill.

Here is the next practical step, because insight without structure does not change a team. Once you understand how failure and learning actually work, you can start noticing what your environment is reinforcing day-to-day. Are your standards pulling people toward excellence, with learning and clarity built in, or are your standards quietly feeding perfection, with fear and hiding built in? That is exactly what the next tool is for. Use the Excellence Decision Matrix below to diagnose what you are unintentionally rewarding, what you are unintentionally punishing, and what you need to shift so your team can sustain high performance without burning out.

The Excellence Decision Matrix: Are We Supporting Excellence, or Feeding Perfection?

It is not enough to say, we want excellence. Leaders have to build the conditions that support it. Otherwise, people default to perfection, not because they want to, but because they are trying to stay safe.

Use the following quick decision matrix to diagnose what you are reinforcing. The top leaders take the time to understand their current state, how they are currently leading to determine the next best steps to take to evolve and grow. That is how they sustain excellence when the pressure never stops.

The Excellence/Perfection Decision Matrix

Decision Area	If you hear or see this, perfection is growing	If you hear or see this, excellence is growing
1. What is driving the standard?	Avoid criticism, avoid blame, make it bulletproof	Serve the purpose, meet the need, uphold our values
2. What does "done" mean?	Done is vague, subjective, or changes person to person	Done is defined in observable outcomes
3. How stable is the bar?	The bar moves weekly, or depends on who is in the meeting	The bar is stable for a season
4. What happens when someone misses the mark?	Shame, silence, punishment, or quiet avoidance	Learning, repair, clarity, and a reset
5. What happens when someone raises a risk or concern?	People learn to stay quiet, or bring it up too late	People are invited to speak early, and are taken seriously
6. What do you reward, really?	Hero mode, overwork, always available, last-minute rescues	Clear priorities, quality choices, healthy boundaries

The decision point, then, is: Are we asking for excellent, and making it possible, or are we asking for perfect, and calling it leadership? Boom! That second question can really sting for the leader with very low self-awareness. It requires a big mirror, one that has been wiped clean and a willingness to being open-eyed in our approach to leading ourselves much more honestly.

I know what it feels like to lose sight of what excellent really looks like and lead from a place of fear. Think back to the merger story in Chapter 2 where I was leading a customer success team and working to transition an entire product line to digital. Not only was the product changing quickly, but so was the cultural sentiment, and the whispers of organizational layoffs. No one was communicating anything to help the troops to drive things forward in a positive way, and the team started guessing. Honestly, I felt my own leadership wobble, and I started to second-guess whether excellent could be possible in the confusion of the environment. Then, I decided to level set what we could control and influence most. I understood that I needed to get my mindset right, and then I could help the entire team get back on track with what was possible despite the current environment. This was my way of stabilizing the canoe. It also helped me name what excellence meant for the season in the chaos of a five-company merger.

If Perfection Is Showing Up, How Leaders Shift the Team Back to Excellence

If perfection is in the room, you do not fix it by telling people to relax. You fix it by giving the team clarity, boundaries, and permission to execute.

Here are practical steps leaders can take to shift from perfection to excellence, without lowering standards. Give it a try. I want you to use this for your specific team.

Step 1: Redefine excellent for this season, in three bullets max

Perfection thrives when excellent is unclear. So name it.

Excellent means:

- ______________________________
- ______________________________
- ______________________________

If it takes more than three bullets, it is too vague to execute. I use this all the time, especially when I am feeling overwhelmed or going in too many directions.

Step 2: Name the tradeoffs out loud and protect them

Excellence always has tradeoffs. Perfection pretends it does not. Say it plainly, here is what we are optimizing for, and here is what we are not optimizing for right now. This is how you remove the hidden pressure that drives burnout. Use the Paddle at the end of this chapter to put pen to paper on this with your team. In the final section of this chapter I will talk more about tradeoffs and boundaries.

Step 3: Build a learning loop, not a hiding loop

Perfection makes people hide mistakes and polish in isolation. Excellence creates a simple learning rhythm: draft, feedback, adjust, ship, debrief. Make it normal to show work early, before it is perfect, so the team can improve together. This is one of my superpowers! I will dive into this more in Zone 2 when I go deeper into psychological safety, but let's just say that normalizing imperfection as your starting point for all things is what gets you and your team to excellence.

Step 4: Remove one load for every new expectation

Saying yes to higher standards without removing anything is not excellence, it is overload.

Protect focus by stopping something, simplifying something, or delaying something.

Tradeoffs are a form of care. I didn't always know this; I learned this the hard way. Some fifteen years ago, I was leading a small team. One day, I had to run out to one of the many meetings I had, but I had a new project to pass to a team member first. Without really thinking about adding one more thing to her plate, I dropped it off and then went on to the meeting. While at the meeting, the stress I'd seen on her face tossed around in my mind. I realized while sitting there that I didn't even ask her what her workload looked like, or whether she could handle one more thing. Immediately following the meeting, I returned to apologize to her and to pause long enough to talk through her list of projects. I helped her move things around and prioritize. This gave her more of a sense of calm.

Step 5: Model steadiness, not obsession

This is where Chapter 1 matters again. A leader who is anxious tends to ask for perfection, even unintentionally. A steady leader can hold the bar without creating fear. I must admit this is hard to do, especially if you aren't self-aware. I can remember on a couple different occasions wanting to double and triple check a presentation before presenting an idea to the executive team. I did so from anxiousness, not from steadiness. In the moment, I didn't realize the fear that type of energy transferred to my team.

Pixar is a useful example here because their creative standard is extremely high, yet their culture is built to support excellence, not perfection. They use a consistent feedback ritual called the Braintrust, where leaders and peers tell the truth about what is not working, early, so the work improves through learning loops instead of hiding loops (Catmull, 2014). That is the difference. Excellence is not about getting it flawless on the first try. Excellence is about building a repeatable system to make it better, together, without shame, without fear, and without grinding people down in the process.

When leaders normalize early drafts, clear standards, and honest feedback, they reduce fear, increase speed, and protect trust. In canoe terms, perfection is paddling in secret and hoping nobody notices the wobble. Excellence is calling the wobble early, adjusting together, and keeping the canoe moving. Once you name excellence, you have to translate it into standards people can hold, not the normal unrealistic ones we see set by many leadership teams. That is how high standards become energizing instead of exhausting.

Standards That Energize Instead of Exhaust

In the previous section, I focused on the difference between perfection and excellence and how you can move your team back to an excellence focus when perfection starts showing up. Here, I want to focus on how you can develop standards that energize your team instead of exhausting them when they are driving for higher levels of performance. Energizing standards can be the stabilizing force your team needs to reach the excellence you want from them. Alternatively, exhausting standards can destabilize the team and put them in the "we can never reach this" mindset.

The following table shows a simple way to think through the two types of standards. As you read through them, think about your own leadership style and your standard-setting habits. Ask yourself: Are the standards I set for my team energizing or exhausting their ability to achieve and sustain high performance? Also, could you personally meet those same standards at the level you expect from them?

Energizing standards feel stabilizing because they are	**Exhausting standards feel destabilizing because they are**
Clear	Vague, just make it great
Stable for a season	Constantly changing
Owned by the team, not just announced by leadership	Measured by personal preference
Paired with resources or time, or an explicit tradeoff	Paired with do more with less
Measured by observable outcomes or behaviors, not opinion	Enforced inconsistently, which feels unfair

Standards are not just a performance tool; they are a trust tool. When people know what is expected, and what success looks like, they stop guessing. Clarity reduces anxiety, and anxiety reduction is a form of care. When you establish team standards, use this thought process. Better yet, include the team in setting and finalizing the standard that you expect them to follow. You will get much more buy-in in the process.

One of the clearest examples of this is one I mentioned earlier in this chapter, Pixar's Braintrust (Catmull, 2014). What made it powerful was not that it was a meeting, it was that it created a shared standard for what "great" looked like, and a consistent, safe way to get there. The feedback was candid, specific, and early, focused on strengthening the work rather than protecting egos, and because the ritual was predictable, teams stopped guessing what would be expected later.

That reduced second guessing, reduced private polishing, and replaced fear with forward motion. In other words, the Braintrust turned excellence into something the team could practice together, not something people had to prove alone. I resonate with this approach in my own leadership. Why set things up where they feel like they are paddling all alone? It is much more energizing to be striving for excellence together.

This matters even more on hybrid and remote teams, where most work happens out of view. If excellence is not defined in writing, people fill in the blanks with assumptions, and assumptions create stress. It also matters when agentic AI is part of the workflow. AI can speed up drafts and analysis, but the team still needs human standards for what quality looks like, what gets reviewed, what cannot be automated, and how you protect trust when tools move fast.

As a longtime leader of teams, I wish I could have had a crystal ball that supplied me with all the right words to say to while I communicated energizing versus exhausting standards to my team. Here are some language examples you can use with your team that I'd like to share with you to minimize your wobble while you search for your own:

- "Here is what excellence looks like in this season."
- "Here is what good looks like, and here is what great looks like."
- "Here is what we are optimizing for right now."
- "Here is what we are not optimizing for right now."
- "Here is what we will do every time, even under pressure."

Obviously, you need to use what works for you in your own style. No matter, excellence requires you to think this through and be prepared to say what resonates with your team in a genuine way and then be sure to align the very next steps to those words.

Those phrases steady the canoe, but they only hold if the shoreline stays stable, and that is where tradeoffs come in, because every standard you set requires you to choose what you will protect, and what you will release.

Tradeoffs and Boundaries: Hold the Bar Without Burning People Out

This chapter is not about whether priorities are clear, you did that work in Chapter 2. This is about what happens when the standard itself becomes a moving target. When leaders keep raising the bar without naming it, when feedback is inconsistent, or when the team is expected to hit quality, speed, scope, responsiveness, and perfection all at once, people start working with a quiet fear of missing the mark.

A team can handle hard work. What breaks people down is hard work plus unclear success plus constantly shifting expectations. That is when excellence turns into never enough. In my Employee Fanatix Team Culture Survey (see the Appendix), role ambiguity and excessive workload show up as repeated contributors to exhaustion, and both are conditions leaders can change by clarifying standards and making real tradeoffs.

When standards are unclear, three silent questions start running in the background of every conversation.

- What does good look like, specifically?
- What does great look like, specifically?
- How will we know we are done?

If you cannot answer those in plain language, people will guess, and guessing is exhausting. If you can answer them, you steady the canoe, because you give the team something stable to paddle toward.

Reflect back on that five-company merger story I referred to earlier where my team and I were also focused on a digital transformation. We were not only responsible for the customer experience, but for getting them to adopt a totally new digital product into their current, mostly paper-focused, process. We worked tirelessly to get our largest clients on board, and then once they would agree with one form of the digital product, the new executive team would request we get buy-in on other changes that served the need of the organization more than it did the customers. Customers were not happy; neither was my team. Morale began to drop. So, I held a meeting with my team to level set what excellent looked like in that moment. I recognized them for their efforts to be agile enough for our organization and patient enough with our upset customers. Simply put, I met them where they were with a bit of empathy and made sure that excellent was defined for the season.

After that meeting, I could see the morale begin to improve, and our customers seemed much more open to the changes as well. I believe it is because the team understood the mission and knew how to talk to the customers about the roll-out in a much clearer way. I committed to meeting them more frequently to be sure they knew what excellence looked like in short order. It is important to state that in that meeting, I also spoke to my team about what projects or items were already on their plates related to the previous set of changes, and I worked with them on what to remove and what to shift. This is steadying because leading your team to stop doing something is also leadership that helps them become more unshakable.

What You Stop Doing Is Leadership

Adopting high standards is likely to add additional load on your team, so failure to subtract an equivalent load of some type creates overload, which points us right back to the signs of burnout and exhaustion I spoke about earlier in this chapter. Leaders earn trust when they protect focus, not just when they inspire effort. Here are several ways for you to protect focus, without guilt:

- Stop meetings that only exist due to habit rather than necessity
- Kill pet projects that no longer match the shoreline
- Simplify requirements, fewer must haves, more clarity
- Delay nonessential work, even if it is popular
- Say no to scope creep, even when it comes from powerful people

I know. That last line, "even when it comes from powerful people" can be a hard one to adopt.

But boundaries are not selfish, they are strategic and tradeoffs are just a form of care for you and your team.

Many years ago, I led a team of client account managers who supported large hospitals and health systems. One day, a senior leader from one of our biggest hospital clients called me out of the blue, clearly frustrated. He told me he wanted his account manager replaced.

I listened, apologized for the experience, and then I said something he did not expect, "I am not changing your account manager."

On the surface, it might sound like I ignored the idea that the customer is always right. But I knew something he either forgot or did not factor in, we had already switched his account manager within the last year for the same reason. If I made the change again, it would have been the easiest path for him, and honestly, the easiest path for me. But it would have taught my team that pressure wins, and people are disposable.

Instead, I coached the account manager, I reset expectations with the client, and I gave her the chance to repair the relationship and grow. My team saw it immediately. That one boundary communicated, I will protect the standard, and I will protect my people while they meet it. The whole team steadied, because they could feel I had their backs, and I was committed to their development, not just the quickest fix. They also got a real-life view into my willingness to make tradeoffs.

Make the Tradeoffs, What You Will Say Yes and No To

Tradeoffs are not time-management, they are identity management. They reveal what you stand for, and what you are willing to protect. The most draining season is when a team is trying to satisfy quality, speed, scope, perfection, and everyone's expectations all at once. No team can hold that for long, which means leaders must choose, then communicate those choices like a shoreline promise.

Tradeoffs your team will run into, and need to name out loud:

- Getting it out fast, versus making it flawless
- Building something custom for one person, versus creating something that works for everyone
- Replying to everything right away, versus protecting time to do the real work
- Keeping everyone happy, versus being clear and setting direction
- Saving the day in the moment, versus building a pace the team can sustain

If everything is urgent, nothing is prioritized. If everything is excellent, nothing is defined. If everything is a yes, the team becomes the cost.

Use the Paddle below as a one-page agreement. When pressure rises, you return to it, together, and it keeps the bar stable for the season. It helps the team stay steady, protect the standard, and avoid burnout.

Paddle: The Excellence Tradeoff Agreement

1. Our definition of excellent, for this season

   Excellent means:

   - ______________________________
   - ______________________________
   - ______________________________

2. What we are focusing on right now

   Choose 1 or 2. For example, speed and clarity, or quality and consistency.

3. What we are not focusing on right now

   Name 1 or 2. For example, perfection, or custom work for every request.

4. Our non-negotiables, the standards we protect no matter what List 2 or 3 behaviors or outcomes. For example, we respond within 24 hours, we give clients weekly updates, we stay under an agreed error threshold.
5. Our tradeoff rules, how we make decisions when we are stretched
   - If it does not serve our top priority, we pause it.
   - If we add something new, we remove something else.
   - If perfection is creeping in, we define what good enough looks like before we keep going.

But even the clearest standards will not hold for long if the team does not trust the leader setting them, or each other enough to raise risks, admit mistakes, and repair quickly when things go wrong. Next, in Chapter 4, we move into Zone 2, The Crew, where trust under pressure becomes the difference between blame that breaks people down and repair that keeps the team steady. Throughout Zone 2, we will build the trust and psychological safety that makes it possible for people to raise risks early, show work before it is polished, and keep the canoe steady together.

Back to the Canoe

Never enough is what happens when excellence is not defined and protected. Define it, protect it, then give the team permission to execute with confidence, not fear.

ZONE

2

The Crew: Trust and Care

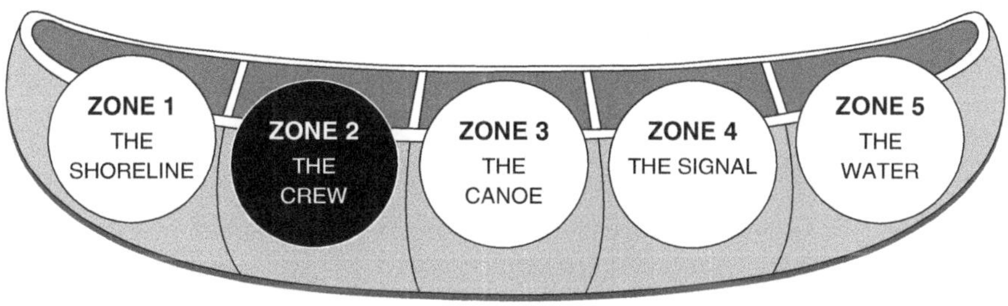

Zone 1 sets the shoreline, but Zone 2 is where the team decides whether they trust the person holding the paddle. Under pressure, trust is the difference between "we have each other" and "every person for themselves." Care is not softness; it is the performance advantage that keeps excellence from turning into exhaustion, and it is how people stay willing to tell the truth early enough to prevent damage.

Chapter 4: Trust Under Pressure: Repair Before Blame

When stress spikes, teams default to protection moves: blame, silence, perfectionism, or side conversations. This chapter teaches leaders how to spot trust leakage early, interrupt blame cycles, and lead repair conversations that restore dignity, accountability, and forward motion.

Chapter 5: Psychological Safety: The Courage to Speak Up

Psychological safety is not comfort; it is permission to be honest before problems become expensive. This chapter shows how leaders create an environment where people raise risks, share bad news, admit mistakes, and challenge ideas without fear, which is exactly what high-performing teams need when the water is rough.

Chapter 6: Belonging: People Perform Where They Feel They Matter

Belonging is the signal that a person's voice has space and their contribution counts, even when the pace is relentless. This chapter focuses on the everyday behaviors that make people feel seen and valued, because people do their best work where they feel safe enough to engage fully and steady enough to stay.

CHAPTER 4

Trust Under Pressure: Repair Before Blame

The first time my son climbed into that canoe with his dad, he was smiling until the shoreline began to slip away. In that instant he realized his safety depended on someone else's paddle. When they returned, he told me he would rather go alone next time so he could make sure he reached the shore. I get it. Many of us feel safer when we are in full control. Yet teams work on a different truth. The minute we step into a shared boat, we choose to trust. We believe the people beside us will pull their weight, keep a steady rhythm, and aim for the same shoreline. That single choice becomes the trigger for what follows: safety, growth, and belonging.

Let me share Sarah's story with you to illustrate this point.

In a high acuity emergency room, Sarah, a veteran nurse, faced one of the most emotionally complex and professionally demanding situations of her career. A pediatric patient was rushed in, barely able to breathe. Sarah jumped into action, her ER training taking over.

But just as she was stabilizing the child, the parent erupted, shouting profanities, demanding she be removed, and refusing to engage calmly.

Now, most people would have frozen or fought back. But Sarah didn't. She took a breath, grounded herself in the moment, and asked a powerful question: "How can I include you in this care, so your child gets what they need?" The parent, still hostile, fired her on the spot.

And here's where the story shifts, where it becomes not just one about personal courage, but about team trust.

Sarah didn't spiral. She didn't try to power through it alone. Instead, she walked out of the room and immediately tapped a teammate on the shoulder: "I've been removed from care. This kid is really sick. I need you to take over." No questions. No judgment. Just support.

Moments later, when the parent threatened to take the child out of the hospital, Sarah stepped back in, still calm, still composed, and convinced them to stay. The child got the critical care they needed, but only because Sarah trusted her team enough to pass the baton.

Looking back, she said, "Early in my career, I wouldn't have been able to do that. But now? I'm proud. I led myself, and I leaned on the team."

Sarah's story is a vivid example of how trust can be the catalyst, the trigger, for climbing into the canoe. She didn't try to row alone. She knew the waters were too rough. And because she had cultivated strong, reciprocal relationships with her team, she could lean on them without hesitation. That moment became more than a patient save. It became a trust building milestone.

As a busy mom of four, I have gone in and out of self-reliance and team reliance. I remember when my children were much younger, I did everything for them, but my husband and I tried to instill some independence in them, we thought for their sake. Later, I realized it was our sake too.

We started with putting together a chore calendar where they would get paid one dollar per chore and then progressively more. Then, as they got older, we only paid them for "mom's chores." So, it was assumed that they would do their part in ordinary ways, but we bonused them on going over and above. This showed all of us the value of recognition for a job well done, and the best way to move the entire canoe forward and keep things running smoothly and with less stress for mom and dad. Our team was a well-oiled machine. We trusted one another to do our parts.

Where in your leadership journey do you need to trust the team more and stop trying to row alone?

I mentioned Caring Leadership in this book's introduction and want to talk a little about that here in the context of building trust and showing concern. In 2021, I wrote *The Art of Caring Leadership*. In it I made a case for why Caring Leadership® is the best way to engage and retain your best people. In that book, I outlined nine specific behaviors that equate to care. My Caring Leadership work always begins with a simple question: Do people feel seen, heard, and valued by you? Trust is how they answer with their actions. When trust is present, people stay, speak up, and stretch. When it is missing, even strong teams drift. Trust is not a speech; it is a pattern of small proofs that repeat over time:

- I do what I said I would do.
- I tell the truth even when it costs me.
- I care about what happens to you, not only what you produce.
- I use my authority to protect, not to punish.

These proofs lower the friction inside a team. With trust we do not waste energy decoding tone or guarding our backs. We surface risks earlier, move faster with clarity, and stretch without burning out because the weight is shared.

I define Caring Leadership as showing concern and kindness to those who look to you for guidance in some way. As I will dive into in a bit, the "who" here includes the leader of the team as well as those they lead. Additionally, to properly show concern and kindness toward your team, you need to do so for yourself first and always, as you learned more about in Chapter 1 on steadying yourself first.

Trust, Defined Simply

My friend, Stephen M. R. Covey, defines trust as "the confidence born of character and competence (Covey, 2008)." I love the short and sweet nature of his definition.

That line matters because it gives you a fast diagnostic in rough waters: when the canoe starts to wobble, people are usually questioning one of two things.

- Character: Can I count on your intent? Will you do what is right, not just what is easy or self-serving?
- Competence: Can I count on your ability? Will you follow through with quality and consistency?

In my work, I translate that into a tool leaders can use in real time: the Wobble Meter is one of those. It helps you notice early warning signs before the boat tips, and it gives you a next best move that repairs trust before blame takes over.

The Wobble Meter: Measure Trust Instantly

Wobble signal you can see or feel	What it often means	Your next best move
Silence, short answers, cameras off, fewer questions	People are protecting themselves. They do not trust the outcome, or they do not trust that it is safe to speak.	Name what you are noticing and invite truth. Ask: "What feels unclear or risky right now?" Then pause long enough for a real answer.
Side conversations, backchanneling, second guessing	Trust is leaking. People are trying to find certainty elsewhere.	Create shared clarity. State the shoreline: the goal, the constraints, and the decision owner. Confirm what will not change.
Over checking, micromanaging, or "Just send it to me" behavior	Competence trust is in question. Someone is not confident work will land.	Reset standards without shame. Agree on what good looks like, define checkpoints, and give ownership back with support.

Wobble signal you can see or feel	What it often means	Your next best move
Defensiveness, blame language, scorekeeping	Character trust is in question. People are protecting reputation instead of protecting the team.	Repair before you debate. Use the Repair Script in the Paddle section. Lead with: "Here's my part. Here's the impact. Here's what I will do next."
Withdrawal, resignation energy, "It doesn't matter anyway"	Trust has been broken or depleted over time.	Make one small promise and keep it fast. Consistency rebuilds faster than speeches. Then close the loop publicly so people see follow-through.

This is an important tool for those who find themselves knee deep in the real world of leading a team through environments with constant pressure as the norm.

What Trust Changes in a Team

Picture a canoe on calm water. With trust, the crew starts together, finds rhythm, and moves almost effortlessly. Without trust, every stroke becomes a correction. We scrape paddles, over steer, and spend precious energy second guessing. Trust reduces that friction so energy can flow into performance and connection.

Our national 2025 Employee Fanatix survey ranked trust among the top three protective factors against burnout. Teams that reported high trust also reported much lower emotional exhaustion, with the effect strongest in remote settings. (See Chart 1 in the Visual Findings of Appendix A.)

You build trust the same way you build endurance: one deliberate practice at a time. Start with the shoreline. Before anyone dips a paddle, name where we are going and how we will know we are still on course. Clarity is a form of care.

Then make and keep small promises. People remember less of our slogans and more of the five-minute follow-up we said we would send and actually sent.

Listen like a teammate, not a judge; paraphrase what you heard, ask the extra question, decode what you hear to make sure you are processing all the helpful angles, act in alignment with what the team needs in the moment and close the loop. Share the paddle by giving real ownership early and visibly so others set the stroke rate on work that affects them.

When you miss, repair quickly. Say what went wrong, name the impact, and outline the fix all from a place of care and steadiness. Repair builds the strength and steadiness you need in your team to sustain excellence.

Remote and Hybrid: Trust at a Distance

Trust gets tested fastest when we are not in the same place. In an office, reliability is visible: you see who shows up, who follows through, and who leans in when something breaks. At a distance, people fill in the blanks with assumptions, and you know they say about assumptions! That is where wobble starts.

When we don't share a physical space, we lose the tiny trust deposits we used to make without thinking: the hallway update, the quick nod after a meeting, the "I'm on it" moment we could see on someone's face. In a distributed world, leaders have to replace accidental reassurance with intentional reliability. Otherwise, silence gets interpreted as avoidance, delayed decisions get interpreted as disrespect, and small misses become narratives.

Here is the shift: don't leave "reliable" to interpretation. Define it, model it, and make it visible through rituals people can count on.

Five Reliability Rituals People Can Feel (Not Just Hear)

- The Monday "What I'm Taking Off Your Plate" Message

  A short note to your team: one priority you're advancing and one burden you're removing. It signals care and traction.

- The Midweek Micro-Update (Two Sentences, Not a Novel)

  "Here's what moved forward. Here's what's stuck and what I need." This prevents guessing games.

- Decision Visibility (So People Don't Have to Chase You)

  A simple shared place where decisions live: what was decided, by whom, and why. Your team does not need more meetings; they need fewer mysteries. This could be put into a spreadsheet that is housed in a Slack channel, and everyone updates it or has access to it. If you have a private intranet site, that could work as well. It's a decision log.

- Response Expectations (So "Fast" Isn't a Personality Test)

  Set humane norms: what's urgent, what can wait, and what channels mean. "Text = urgent. Email = within 24–48." Reliability becomes shared language.

- The Friday Close-the-Loop Habit

  End the week with: "What I delivered, what I learned, what I'm carrying into next week." This is how trust stays intact across time zones.

A helpful modern example comes from Atlassian. They formalized a distributed approach called "Team Anywhere," allowing employees to choose where they work while intentionally building distributed norms. In their published learnings after implementing Team Anywhere, they reported no drop-off in work activity and shared practical lessons from extended distributed work (Farquhar, 2021). The leadership takeaway is not "copy their model," but copy the principle: when proximity disappears, you make reliability more visible through clear commitments, transparent decisions, and consistent follow-through.

Distributed teams need visible signals of reliability that feel human, not robotic. It is less about having more meetings and more about making small promises and keeping them in a way others can see.

I have a small, fully remote, team. That is the only way I have operated since 2017, when I formed the company. My team all knew their role was remote. I never put pressure on them to have any other way of working. Early on, I would wonder why one team member did not respond to a Slack message right away. I'd be lying if I said that I didn't wonder if they were at the spa or hanging with a friend. They may have sensed some of my hesitation or even lack of trust, but then we started to put together ground rules on the maximum time it would take for any of us to respond to one another and even the best two ways to communicate if something was urgent. Once we established this cadence, my anxiousness dissipated, and I would guess theirs did too.

In a podcast interview with Tracy Nolan, Senior Vice President, MarketPoint, we explored what caring leadership looks like when it has backbone, when expectations are clear, accountability is real, and compassion does not disappear under pressure. The takeaway was simple: leaders do not have to choose between being human and getting results. The strongest cultures build both, because people do not burn out from high standards; they burn out from high standards without care.

Looking at my personal story above, it's clear to me that every team member reporting to me perceives that I have high standards. They also perceive that I hold myself to the same high standards. That said, my team will tell you that I also lead them with great care. I have never felt that I needed to lower my standards in exchange for treating them like my partners on this journey to impact. I care about them deeply. I concede that I also want the projects completed on time and with as much precision as possible. I can have and be both. So can you. Over my years leading teams through change, stress, and mounting expectations, I can only think of a few when trust was broken, either by them or by me. In each case, the canoe wobbled and we needed to repair trust to stabilize it again.

Repairing Trust: The Fastest Way to Steady the Canoe After a Wobble

Trust is not fragile because people make mistakes. Trust breaks when people pretend the mistake did not happen, minimize the impact, or move on without repairing what the miss created. Under pressure, leaders sometimes avoid the repair conversation because they think it will slow things down. But avoiding it is what slows everything down later. The unspoken tension starts steering the canoe. People become cautious, they stop raising risks, they protect themselves, and suddenly you are leading a team that is busy, but not fully with you.

Repair is a leadership skill. It is also a form of care. When a leader can name their part, name the impact, and name the fix, it tells the team, "we do not have to be perfect here, we do have to be honest here." That is how you protect momentum without sacrificing trust.

In healthy teams, repair is normal, not dramatic. It is not a big apology tour. It is a short, steady reset that clears the air and gets everyone back in rhythm. Think of it like this, when the canoe wobbles, you do not punish the wobble, you correct the stroke and re-center the weight so you can keep moving forward.

Use the script below anytime you sense tension rising, when a miss happens, or when you realize you have been unclear, inconsistent, or unavailable. The goal is not to overexplain. The goal is to restore clarity and connection so the team can keep paddling together.

When you feel the wobble, do not wait for a blowup. Repair before blame. Return to character and competence, and use the Repair Script. Trust is the trigger. Use it early and often, and watch psychological safety, growth, and belonging follow.

Paddle: The Repair Script

Use this when tension rises, a miss happens, or the canoe starts to wobble. Keep it short; say it with steadiness.

1. Name your part. "Here is what I did, or what I did not do."
2. Name the impact. "Here is how I think it affected you, or the team."
3. Name the fix. "Here is what I will do next, and by when."
4. Invite partnership. "What do you need from me so we can move forward?"
5. Close the loop. "I will circle back on date and tell you what changed."

Repair builds trust, but trust deepens even more when people know they can speak up before the damage is done. In Chapter 5, we move into psychological safety, the courage to speak up, where the team learns that honesty, questions, and early risk raising are not dangerous acts, but essential ones.

Back to the Canoe

Trust is the invisible rhythm that keeps two paddlers moving as one. When it wobbles, you do not pretend it did not happen, you repair, you reset the stroke, and you keep paddling together with steadiness and care.

CHAPTER

5

Psychological Safety: The Courage to Speak Up

Psychological safety is the difference between a team that can navigate rough water and a team that looks steady until it tips. In this chapter we are talking about the courage to tell the truth when it matters.

Amy Edmondson, the Harvard professor most associated with this research, defines psychological safety as "a shared belief held by members of a team that the team is safe for interpersonal risk taking (Edmondson, 2018)." In plain language, it means people believe they can speak up, ask questions, name concerns, admit mistakes, and offer ideas, without being punished, dismissed, or embarrassed.

This is not about being nice. It is not about lowering standards. Psychological safety is what allows high standards to work, especially under pressure. When psychological safety is strong, teams surface risks earlier, solve problems faster, and recover from mistakes without spiraling into blame. When it is weak, people stay quiet, and silence becomes a performance problem.

Why It Matters in a Canoe

In a canoe, a small shift changes the ride for everyone. The water moves, the wind changes, fatigue sets in, and one person's wobble becomes the whole team's wobble. The safest teams are not the teams with zero wobble. They are the teams that name the wobble early, adjust together, and keep paddling. Psychological safety is what makes that possible.

When the water gets rough, teams do not need tougher people. They need safer leadership, leadership that makes it normal to say, I am not sure, I see a risk, I disagree, I made a mistake, I need help, before the wobble becomes a tip.

Silence Is Expensive

When psychological safety is low, people do not stop having concerns. They stop sharing them. That is when teams drift into preventable mistakes, delayed decisions, rework, resentment, and burnout.

Silence often looks like this:

1. People nod in meetings, then disagree later in side conversations.
2. Risks get raised late, when it is almost too late to course correct.
3. Mistakes get hidden, then they get bigger.
4. Strong people disengage because it feels safer to stay quiet than to contribute.

This is why psychological safety is not a soft topic. It is a performance topic. It is also a care topic, because when people feel unsafe to speak, their nervous system stays on alert. Constant self-protection is exhausting, but as a leader of the team, you have the power to make psychological safety normalized in everyday interactions.

If you want a vivid example of psychological safety in action, look at my earlier example of NASA's Apollo 13 mission. In April 1970, an oxygen tank exploded, and the mission shifted instantly from landing on the moon to getting three astronauts home alive. NASA Mission Control faced a fast moving, high-stakes crisis with limited options and no room for ego (NASA History Office, 2011).

What mattered in that moment was not just technical expertise; it was the willingness to surface problems, challenge assumptions, and say the hard thing early. Engineers had to speak up about what would not work. Flight directors had to ask questions they wished they did not have to ask. Teams had to share partial ideas, iterate quickly, and make decisions without perfect information. One of the clearest examples of disciplined teamwork under pressure was the improvised carbon dioxide filter solution. The crew's square CO_2 canisters had to fit into a round system, and rising carbon dioxide levels made it urgent. Engineers on the ground and astronauts in the capsule worked the problem with what they already had on board, proving that under stress, and in a true pressure situation, the team that survives is the team that tells the truth fast, without fear.

That is psychological safety. It is not comfort. It is a shared commitment to reality, paired with enough trust that people can take interpersonal risks for the sake of the mission.

In the work I do to support leadership teams and employees through my culture work, this lack of safety is the thing I see most. In fact, I'd venture to say I would have very little culture transformation work to do if all leadership teams made psychological safety a real, lived thing in their environments. Most often, they bring me in because the frontline doesn't trust their leaders enough to tell them the *real* truth. So, they tell me the truth, and then I package it in a way that the leadership team can not only understand but accept and act upon. My mere presence in those listening sessions sends an important message from senior leaders to their employees: "We know we have lost your trust, and we'd like to show you that we want to earn it back." I am always humbled by how seen and appreciated the employees are when we complete our sessions. They have a glimmer of hope that using their voices will lead to positive change and more safety in the future.

Trust and Care at the Foundation

Trust is the belief that I can rely on you. Care is the belief that you will treat me like a person while we do the work. Psychological safety is the belief that my voice is welcome here.

When leaders show steadiness, keep commitments, and repair quickly when they miss, trust grows. When leaders stay curious, listen without punishing, and protect dignity, care becomes visible. When trust and care show up consistently, people take the risk of speaking up. Steady leadership builds trust. Caring leadership protects dignity. Together, they create safety.

That is the chain, and it takes me right back to my son in that canoe.

What I watched in him that day was not just nerves about the water. It was the moment he realized, I am not in control of everything, and I have to trust the people in this boat. That is a vulnerable feeling. And vulnerability is exactly what most people avoid at work. People would rather stay silent than risk looking wrong, looking slow, or looking like they need help. But silence does not keep the canoe steady. It just hides the imbalance until the water gets rough.

That is where leadership comes in. A steady, caring leader makes that risk safer. They create an environment where it is normal to say, I do not understand, I disagree, I made a mistake, I need support, without losing respect. Now let's get specific about the behaviors leaders use to create that kind of safety.

Leader Behaviors That Create Safety

Psychological safety is not created by telling people, you can speak up here. It is created by what happens the first time someone actually does. Here is a side-by-side view of what this kind of safety does and does not look like, in practice.

Leaders create safety when they	Leaders destroy safety when they
Respond to bad news with curiosity, not heat	Punish messengers, even subtly
Ask for input before a decision is final	Use sarcasm or public correction
Thank people for raising risks early	Act like questions are inconvenience
Separate the person from the problem	Reward agreement and label dissent as negativity
Repair quickly when they miss	Say, "bring me solutions only," when people are trying to raise risks
Make it normal to say, I do not know yet, and then follow up	Expect and accept only one "right" answer

As a longtime mid-level leader of teams, I have seen many of the unsafe behaviors above unfold in big meetings and in one-on-ones. I have also seen the impact of a psychologically unsafe leader on the culture more times than I hope to admit. When people don't feel safe enough to speak up and present a different opinion than the majority of folks in the room, the results can be damaging.

Let's reflect back to Apollo 13 and imagine the same crisis without psychological safety. You already know how high the stakes were, and how quickly Mission Control had to move with incomplete information. Now picture a different culture in that room.

Engineers hesitate to raise concerns because they do not want to sound negative. Someone notices a risk but waits until they have a perfect solution before speaking. A flight controller is afraid to challenge the room because the most senior voice already chose a direction. A junior person sees a problem, but assumes it is not their place to say it out loud.

In that version of the story, the problem is not the explosion; it is the silence that follows it. Decisions slow down, bad assumptions live longer, and the team wastes precious time protecting egos instead of protecting lives. Psychological safety is what allows a team to say, I see a risk, I do not think this will work, here is what we are missing, without fear of being punished for telling the truth. It keeps the room focused on reality, not reputation. In canoe terms, the water got dangerous, and the only way through was truth, fast, from everyone, not just the loudest voice.

No Safety Without Curiosity

Psychological safety cannot grow in a room where the leader shows up as the person with all the answers. When leaders enter meetings in solution mode, they often skip the most important part, understanding what is actually happening. Curiosity is what makes it safe for other people to tell the truth. It signals, you are not going to be punished for raising a risk, you are not going to be dismissed for having a different view, and you are not going to be labeled as difficult for asking a hard question.

Curiosity also protects leaders from a common pressure reflex, certainty. Under stress, certainty feels efficient. It feels strong. But a leader's certainty can quietly shut down the room. People start editing themselves, waiting to be told what to do, or staying silent until it is too late. Curiosity does the opposite. It invites early information, it surfaces assumptions, and it creates shared ownership of the problem, which is exactly what teams need in dangerous waters.

I like to think of curiosity as my willingness to be changed by what is around me and by what others in the room say.

Here are four very important curiosity moves that create safety:

1. Presence, without rushing to fix

   Start by making space for what you do not yet know. Try saying, "Walk me through what you are seeing," or "Help me understand what is hardest right now."

2. Clarity, by naming assumptions out loud

   Curiosity is not endless discussion. It is disciplined understanding. Try saying, "What are we assuming is true," "What do we know for sure," and "What would change our mind."

3. Boundaries with exploration, not boundaries with shutdown

   Safety requires clarity about what is open for input, and what is not. Try saying, "Here is what is decided," "Here is what is still open," and "Here is the one question I need answered before we move."

4. Normalize them calling out your mistakes

Psychological safety becomes the norm when you make your misunderstanding the center of the conversation. Try saying, "What about what I just presented as the solution will not work at all?" Or "Where is my thinking flawed."

If you want your team to speak up, the fastest shift you can make is this: walk into the room curious. It changes the air. It gives people permission to contribute, and it turns leadership from a monologue into a steady dialogue that keeps the canoe upright.

As a leader, this has always been one of my strengths. Here is my simple philosophy: I surround myself with the smartest people I can find. Since I know there are really smart people in the room, I expect them to use their strengths to steady the entire team's mission. I will often ask them to shoot holes in my thinking, because if they can't find things wrong with my thinking, then it is usually a solid starting point. If they can find holes and advise me against any one course of action, I often let them overrule the solution that I thought was sound to start.

Use this paddle when pressure rises, when meetings get tense, or when you sense people pulling back.

Paddle: The Safety Behaviors Checklist: Meeting Norms That Protect Truth Telling

1. Set the expectation.

Say, "I want risks raised early, questions asked out loud, and dissent surfaced respectfully."

2. Normalize not knowing.

Say, "If you are uncertain, say so, we will figure it out together."

3. Make room for quieter voices first.

Say, "Let's hear from someone who has not spoken yet."

4. Respond to concerns with curiosity.

   Say, "Say more, what are you seeing, what is the risk, what would you recommend."

5. Turn input into action.

   Say, "Here is what we are doing because of what you raised, and here is what we are not doing, and why."

6. Protect dignity in the moment.

   No sarcasm, no eye rolling, no public shaming, no piling on.

7. Close with clarity.

   Say, "Here is what we decided, why we decided it, and who owns what next."

Psychological safety gives people the courage to speak, but belonging is what helps them believe they truly have a place in the conversation and on the team. In Chapter 6, we move into belonging, being wanted, not just tolerated, where trust and safety become something even deeper: the steady knowledge that your presence, your voice, and your contribution truly matter.

Back to the Canoe

In rough water, the most dangerous thing is not the wave, it is the silence. When people trust that their voice will be met with steadiness and care, they call the wobble early, adjust together, and keep the canoe upright. That is what psychological safety gives a team, the courage to tell the truth in time.

CHAPTER

6

Belonging: People Perform Where They Feel They Matter

"Wanted" is invitation. It is the feeling that your presence is not an inconvenience. You are not being managed around. You are being brought in, and people want you in the same place and space as they are.

Leaders show their team members that they are wanted when they:

1. Notice someone who has gone quiet
2. Check in when effort is high but the energy is dropping
3. Invite someone into the room where the work is shaped
4. Make it normal to ask for help and offer help
5. Protect dignity in front of others, especially under pressure

Leader language that signals wanted:

1. "I want you in this conversation early, before we decide."
2. "Your view matters here, what am I missing?"
3. "I know this is messy; we will figure it out together."
4. "I see the effort, what support would make this more workable?"

In canoe terms, wanted is what keeps a newer paddler from shrinking in their seat. It tells them, you belong on this crew, and we are paying attention to whether you can keep paddling sustainably.

I call this "inviting people into the circle." I am an only child. So, I remember as a kid often feeling like an outsider or like I was lonely. It is often said that pain is a great teacher, and I used that early pain to define a part of how I'd show up. When I saw someone sitting alone in the cafeteria, I would invite them into my group or just go and sit with them. I remember in law school there was one guy who just read by himself in the hallway. I hated that he was always on the outside. So, I would always invite him into my circles and ask him to tell us his opinion when he was quiet. He was brilliant! I am so glad I called on him to speak. On multiple occasions, he helped me see another way around an issue. I have found that the quietest person in the room often has the most profound ways to contribute. I am usually the catalyst to invite them in. I do this because I want them to know that I want them there, with me and in my circle.

The last elements of my belonging definition are appreciation and being valued. Both are powerful tools to sustain excellence over time.

Belonging Is Appreciated and Valued, People Know Their Contribution Counts

Being appreciated and valued is not flattery. It is recognition and fairness people can feel. This is where leaders turn care into something visible, and trust into something consistent.

Research backs this up. In a BetterUp study, employees who felt a strong sense of belonging, versus a weak one, experienced a 56% increase in job performance (BetterUp, 2019). That is not about compliments. That is what happens when people can stop scanning for signals of unfairness, stop guessing what counts, and start putting their full attention on doing great work. Belonging shows up when a person can feel, through real decisions and everyday leadership behaviors, that their contribution counts.

Let me share a personal story with you that perfectly illustrates this point. When I first took over a team of eclectic customer experience reps, I walked into a group that was talented and committed, but also a little guarded and subdued. They were working hard, yet you could feel the stress in the air, not because they did not care, but because they were not fully sure what great meant from one week to the next, or whether their effort would be recognized fairly.

I will be honest, at first, I tried to solve it the way many leaders do; I worked harder, communicated more, and jumped in quickly to help when things felt wobbly. But the more I pushed, the more I noticed people second guessing, staying quiet in meetings, and over polishing work just to be safe. That was my wake-up call. I realized the team did not need more intensity from me. They needed more steadiness, and they needed proof that their contribution counted.

So, I slowed down and made three things visible: opportunity, feedback, and recognition. I got clear about what responsibilities truly mattered in this season. I made stretch work and visibility more intentional. I tightened our feedback so people were not guessing what success looked like. And I started recognizing specific contributions in real time so the team could feel what good and great actually meant.

The shift was not instant perfection, and I had to keep checking my own habits, but the team's energy changed. People stopped scanning for hidden rules. They spoke up sooner. They delivered better work with less friction, because they finally felt like they had a place, a voice, and a leader who was committed to making excellence possible, not just demanding it.

When leaders do appreciation well, they reduce the quiet question people ask under pressure: "Does my contribution matter, or am I just a body in a seat?" And one of the clearest ways people answer that question is through whether leadership feels fair and consistent, especially in opportunity, feedback, and recognition.

People feel valued when they see fairness in three areas:

1. Opportunity: who gets stretch work, visibility, and meaningful responsibilities
2. Feedback: who gets coached, who gets clarity, who gets the truth early
3. Recognition: who gets credit, and what behaviors get celebrated (more on this below)

This does not mean everyone gets the same thing. It means the process is consistent enough that people do not have to wonder if contribution matters, or if proximity and preference matter more. The final element of my definition of Belonging includes showing deep appreciation.

Genuine Appreciation as a Belonging Stabilizer

Genuine appreciation is one of the fastest ways to make belonging real, and I want to be clear what I mean by that, because appreciation is not flattery and it is not forced positivity. Genuine appreciation is when a leader makes someone's contribution visible in a way that feels accurate, specific, and earned. It is the difference between "Great job, team" and "The way you handled that client escalation protected trust and reduced churn, and I want you to know I saw it."

This matters because when pressure rises, people start scanning for safety and fairness. They scan for whether effort matters. They scan for whether leaders notice what is real or only what is loud. If the environment is uncertain, appreciation becomes even more stabilizing, because it reminds people, "My work still counts here."

Gallup puts real numbers behind this. Employees are four times as likely to be engaged when they strongly agree they receive the right amount of recognition for the work they do (Lorenz, 2022). Engagement is not a nice-to-have. It is capacity. It is energy. It is someone deciding, "I'm still in this canoe with you."

There is another layer leaders miss. Appreciation is not just about gratitude; it is also about strengths. When people get to use what they naturally do well, they feel more confident, more useful, and more rooted. Gallup research has found that employees who use their strengths every day are six times more likely to be engaged at work and three times more likely to report having an excellent quality of life (Robison, 2020). That is belonging in action. People perform where they feel they matter, and one of the clearest ways they feel that is when their strengths are seen, named, and used on purpose.

So, if you want a practical gut check as a leader, ask yourself this:

Are my people only hearing from me when something goes wrong, or are they also hearing from me when they are doing what "excellent" looks like in real time?

Because if people only get attention when there is a problem, belonging becomes conditional, and conditional belonging always creates wobble.

This reminds me of a conversation I had with a senior leader from a large law firm, someone I met on a flight during a season when his firm was moving through an acquisition. He told me something I have never forgotten. He said the acquisition itself was not what broke people. What broke people was the silence, the guessing, and the feeling that leadership was hiding behind email while expecting everyone to keep producing like nothing was happening.

He said, "People are adults. They can handle the truth in parts. They just cannot handle being treated like they cannot handle it."

That line has stayed with me because it captures what so many leaders get wrong during change. They say, "We cannot share much right now," and that may be legally true. But then they go quiet, and quiet creates a vacuum, and vacuums get filled with fear. Meanwhile, leaders still need the team to show up, still need extra effort, still need someone to come in on a weekend and push a case over the finish line.

Here is what he told me made the difference in his world. The leaders who kept loyalty did not rely on drive by announcements or last-minute pressure. They stayed present. They told people what they could, when they could, and they acknowledged what they could not yet say without acting like the team was fragile. They also practiced appreciation in small, specific ways that made people feel seen while the ground was shifting.

He described leaders writing short notes, leaving a sticky note on someone's desk after a hard week, calling out real contributions in front of peers, ordering in food when the team was working late, and most importantly, walking the floor and saying, "I see what this is costing you, and I'm grateful you are still here paddling with us."

Then he said something that hit me straight in the belonging nerve. He said, "When leaders do not build allegiance before they need it, they should not be surprised when people refuse the weekend ask."

That is the belonging lesson inside change. The request for buy-in only lands when the relationship already carries trust and dignity. You cannot treat people like interchangeable labor Monday through Thursday and then ask for devotion on Saturday. Belonging is what makes extra effort possible without resentment. Appreciation is one of the ways belonging becomes visible.

If you want to turn that into leader language you can actually use, here is what it sounds like:

- "I can't share everything yet, but I can share what I know today, and I can promise you we will not disappear."
- "I know this is not comfortable. I'm not going to pretend it is."
- "Here is what I need this weekend, and here is what I'm doing to make sure this ask is not the new normal."
- "I want to acknowledge what you have carried this week. I see it, and it matters."

That is how you build buy-in without manipulation. You respect people enough to tell the truth in parts, and you appreciate them enough to make their effort visible while the water is rough.

Remote, Hybrid, and Agentic AI Workflows: Belonging Must Be Designed

This matters even more on hybrid and remote teams, where most work happens out of view. If excellence is not defined in writing, people fill in the blanks with assumptions, and assumptions create stress. Belonging can also erode faster when you are not in the same room, because visibility and voice are easier to lose.

A simple way to protect belonging at a distance is to make three things explicit:

1. What matters most this week and how their specific job function contributes to that. This can be done on weekly team calls and even be documented in a Slack stream.
2. Who owns what, and where decisions will be made. Use Teams or Slack channels to manage this. Later in this book, I review decision rights and provide tools for making this explicit.
3. What good looks like, in writing, not in vibes (intentional recognition or a job well done).

It also matters when agentic AI is part of the workflow. AI can speed up drafts and analysis, but the team still needs human standards for what quality looks like, what gets reviewed, what cannot be automated, and how credit is shared so contribution does not become invisible.

When people feel replaceable, or uncredited, or reduced to prompt and paste, belonging drops. When leaders protect clarity, voice, and visible contribution, belonging holds, even as tools move fast.

Captain David Marquet presents a great case study for us regarding what an intentional belonging system can look like. When Captain

4. Valued check

Ask, who has carried heavy work lately, and have I made their contribution visible?

Make one move this week. Choose one person to give clearer ownership, one place to invite earlier voice, and one contribution to recognize in a specific way.

Belonging is the human anchor that keeps people engaged when the work is hard, but even the most connected team will start to wobble if the way work gets done is unclear or unstable. In Zone 3, we shift into the operating system of the team, the roles, standards, and structure that reduce hidden drag, and Chapter 7 starts by making ownership unmistakable so the canoe stays steady when pressure rises.

Back to the Canoe

In rough water, a crew cannot afford "insiders" and "outsiders"—every paddler's voice is a stabilizer. Belonging is what keeps people in rhythm, and when rhythm holds, the canoe moves farther with less strain.

ZONE 3

The Canoe: Systems and Structure

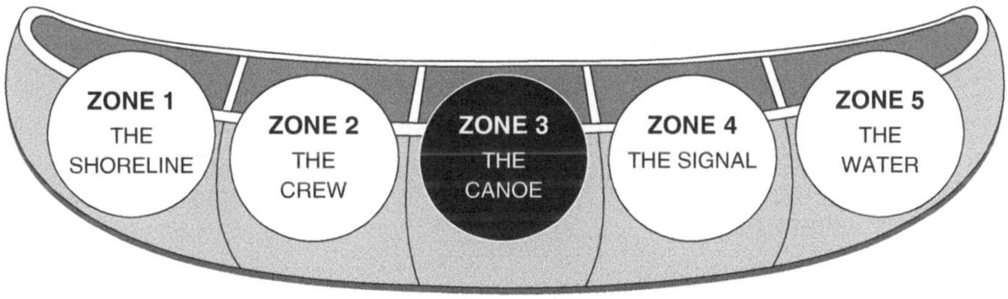

Zone 3 is your operating system. It is roles, standards, decision rights, and the rhythm of how work actually gets done. If the canoe is unstable, even strong performers start compensating, double checking, reworking, stepping on each other, or going quiet. But when the canoe is solid, the team can put their energy into forward motion instead of bracing for impact.

In this Zone, we are going to take the "invisible wobble" and make it visible, so you can fix it before it becomes expensive.

Chapter 7: Stabilize the Canoe: Roles That Reduce Wobble

Most teams do not have a talent problem; they have a role clarity problem. In this chapter, you will learn how unclear ownership creates drag, frustration, and blame, and how clear roles create steadiness. You will build roles in a way that makes handoffs cleaner, expectations fairer, and trust easier to sustain, especially when pressure rises.

Chapter 8: Decision Rights: Who Decides What, When

When teams wobble, a lot of the time it is not because people disagree, it is because no one is sure who gets to decide. This chapter helps you eliminate decision fog by defining decision rights in plain language, tightening escalation paths, and reducing the delays and second guessing that quietly exhaust people. Clarity here is not control; it is capacity protection.

Chapter 9: The Operating Rhythm: Meetings and Rituals That Protect Capacity and Focus

Even with the right people and clear decisions, teams can still burn out if the day-to-day cadence is chaotic. In this chapter, you will design a rhythm that keeps the work moving without grinding people down. You will learn how to use meetings and rituals as stabilizers, how to reduce noise and duplication, and how to protect deep work, recovery, and follow-through so excellence stays sustainable.

CHAPTER

7

Stabilize the Canoe: Roles That Reduce Wobble

In Zone 1, we set the Shoreline—purpose, priorities, standards, and tradeoffs. In Zone 2, we built the human conditions that keep teams steady—trust, safety, and belonging. Now we enter Zone 3, the Canoe itself, the systems and structure that keep the work from wobbling when pressure rises.

Teams do not burn out only from workload. They burn out from unclear work. When roles are fuzzy, people spend energy translating, guessing, double checking, and trying not to step on each other. That is the wobble. And it is sneaky because it can look like effort. Everyone is busy, meetings are full, tasks are getting done, but ownership is missing.

This chapter is about ownership, and the roles that empowerment, delegation, and accountability play in making ownership a reality. Decision rights matter too, and we will go deeper on them in the next chapter. For now, here is the stabilizing truth. Ownership is not an attitude. It is an agreement that has many components.

What "Owning It" Actually Means

When teams say, "own it," they usually mean "care more." But ownership is not only caring more. Ownership is making the outcome real, end to end, for one human being.

Owning it means five practical things, without corporate jargon:

1. I own the outcome, not just the tasks.
2. I name what I need from others early, not at the deadline.
3. I make progress visible in a way others can count on.
4. I surface risks when they are still small.
5. I close the loop, I do not leave people guessing.

When ownership is clear, work moves forward with less friction. When ownership is unclear, work still happens, but it happens sideways. People do pieces, they stay busy, they respond to pings, but nobody can confidently steer.

Once you see ownership clearly, the next question becomes obvious. How do you actually build it on purpose instead of hoping it shows up through effort and good intentions? That is where empowerment, delegation, accountability, and buy-in come in. They are not separate leadership topics; they are the infrastructure that turns ownership into something real and repeatable. Ownership is the destination. Empowerment and delegation are how you hand someone the paddle with clarity. Accountability is how you keep the canoe moving in the same direction once the handoff happens, and buy-in is how you make sure people are not just rowing because you told them to, but because they understand what we are protecting and what winning looks like in this season.

Empowerment Without Chaos, Delegation with Dignity, Accountability That Does Not Feel Like Punishment

If you want an unshakable team, you cannot build it on heroics. You build it on clarity. This is where empowerment, delegation, accountability, and buy-in stop being leadership buzzwords and start becoming the operating system of the canoe.

A lot of leaders say they want empowered teams, but what they really mean is, I want you to take initiative, but I also want you to do it exactly the way I would do it. That is not empowerment. That is anxiety with a title.

Empowerment is not the absence of leadership. Empowerment is the presence of clear decision rights, clear standards, and a clear shoreline. It is you saying, here is what we are trying to accomplish, here is what we must protect, here is what good looks like, and here is what you own. Then you actually let them own it.

In canoe terms, empowerment is not you dropping the paddle in someone's lap and hoping they figure it out mid-current. It is you giving them the paddle with three things in place: direction, rhythm, and trust. Direction is the outcome. Rhythm is the check-in cadence. Trust is the belief that they can carry it, and that you will not yank the paddle back the moment the water gets choppy.

Delegation is the bridge between your intent and their reality. When delegation is vague, people fill in the blanks with stress. When delegation is clear, people fill in the blanks with competence. Delegation is giving someone the ability to step into the shoes of another person to do their job. Empowerment is about self-actualization, providing access to someone to perform their work in the way that helps them meet their highest potential.

Here is the simplest way I know to delegate in a way that protects performance and reduces wobble:

- Start with the outcome. What does success look like in plain language.
- Name the boundaries. What must not be compromised. Time, quality, budget, safety, brand, relationships, compliance. Pick the few that truly matter.

- Clarify the decision rights. Are they recommending, deciding, or executing. This is where so much frustration and rework comes from. People think they own a decision when they only own a draft, or they assume they do not have authority when you actually wanted them to decide. More on this in the next chapter.
- Provide the resources or the tradeoff. If you want excellent outcomes, you have to make it possible. If something new is being added, something else has to be paused, simplified, or delayed. Otherwise you are not delegating, you are stacking weight.
- Set the rhythm. When do we check-in? How will you surface risks early? What is the definition of done?

If you do that, you will notice something powerful. Accountability stops feeling like pressure and starts feeling like clarity. People know what they own, they know how success will be measured, and they know the support is real. That is how you keep excellence from turning into exhaustion.

Accountability is not micromanagement. Accountability is follow-through. It is the steady leader saying, we agreed, and I intend to honor what we agreed to, and I expect you to honor it too. That is not harsh. That is caring. Because when accountability is absent, the strongest people carry the weakest systems, and resentment becomes the current nobody wants to name.

There is also an emotional side to this that leaders often miss. Empowerment requires a leader who can tolerate wobble. Because the moment you empower someone, they will do some things differently than you would. They might be slower at first. They might ask questions you think they should already know. They might make a decision you would not have made. If your nervous system interprets that as danger, you will unconsciously claw back control. You will hover. You will rewrite their work. You will "just take it from here," and the team will learn the lesson quickly: ownership is not safe here.

This is why Zone 1 matters even inside Zone 3. If you cannot steady yourself in the middle of delegation, you will accidentally train your team to depend on you and dependence looks like alignment until the day you are not available, and then the canoe tips.

Now let's talk about buy-in. Buy-in is not compliance. It is ownership of the outcome. And you do not get ownership by announcing decisions. You get ownership by involving people early enough that their voice can actually shape something. I'll talk a lot about this in Zone 4.

Sometimes, you will not be able to give everyone a vote. That is real life, but you can almost always give people a voice. When you do, you reduce resistance because you reduce the story that leadership is hiding something. The key is to be honest about what is open and what is not.

Here is language you can use that builds buy-in without pretending:

"We are solving for this outcome, here is what is non-negotiable, and here is what we can shape together. I want your input before we finalize."

Then, when the decision is made, close the loop. That is where trust is either built or lost. Tell them what you heard, what you chose, what you did not choose, and why. Even when people do not love the outcome, they can tolerate it better when the process feels dignified.

This takes me back to a team leader I worked with, someone I trusted deeply, and she knew it. At one point, I empowered her to take over our team meetings and design the experience from start to finish, because I already knew she was great at creating rhythm and connection. What I did not expect was how personally she would take it. She thought through each team member's communication style and what helped them feel comfortable contributing. She added small, customized touches that made people want to show up, engage, and feel seen while doing it.

That experience taught me something I still come back to. When I released the need to control something that honestly was not a big deal for me, but it clearly mattered to her, she created something better than anything I would have designed myself. I was clear about what I needed the meetings to accomplish, then I gave her space to do it her way, and she absolutely knocked it out of the park.

The bottom line is this. Empowerment is not a nice-to-have. Delegation is not a favor. Accountability is not a weapon. These are structural stabilizers. They reduce drag, reduce wobble, and keep the canoe moving in rhythm, even when the water gets loud. Next let's look at how roles are important to the concept of ownership.

The Five Signs of Role Wobble

Role wobble usually shows up in predictable patterns. You can use this as a quick diagnostic in kickoffs, handoffs, and recurring meetings, and you can name the hidden cost associated with the wobble.

The 5 D's of Role Wobble	What it looks like in real life	The hidden cost
Duplication	Two people unknowingly work the same problem	Time lost, morale drops, frustration rises
Drift	Work gets done, but not toward the same outcome	Misalignment, rework, missed targets
Delay	Decisions stall because nobody is sure who owns the result	Slow execution, endless meetings
Diffusion	Responsibility spreads so thin that accountability disappears	"Someone should" replaces "I will"
Drain	High performers carry the confusion and quietly burn out	Retention risk, resentment, uneven load

Role wobble is not just annoying; it is expensive. Research consistently shows that role ambiguity tracks with higher burnout and stronger intent to leave, and in meta-analytic work it emerges as a meaningful predictor alongside other stressors (Kim and Kim, 2021). In other words, when roles stay fuzzy, people do not simply get slower, they get more depleted, and the organization quietly absorbs the cost through rework, friction, and retention risk.

Role Clarity as Burnout Prevention

Role clarity is not bureaucracy. It is the fastest way to remove unnecessary friction. Under pressure, unclear outcomes create drift. Unclear owners create polite accountability. Unclear update rhythms create late surprises. Every one of those wobbles carries a real cost, not just in time and efficiency, but in trust. People start thinking, "If we cannot even name who owns what, how will we handle the hard stuff when the water gets rough?"

Use this four-question check-in for kickoffs, handoffs, and recurring meetings. If you cannot answer them in simple language, you are not ready to ask the team to paddle harder.

If the answer is unclear, the canoe wobbles. If the answer is clear, the canoe steadies.

Role clarity question	If the answer is unclear, the canoe wobbles	If the answer is clear, the canoe steadies
Outcome: What are we trying to deliver, in observable terms	People do activity instead of delivery	People can aim together
Owner: Who is responsible for the result	Accountability gets polite and vague	Accountability becomes kind and direct
Signals: How will we track progress, and when do we update	Surprises show up late	Risks show up early
Support: Who do we need, and by when	Dependencies ambush the timeline	Help shows up on time

Apollo 13 is a powerful reminder of what role clarity makes possible when the stakes are high. After the explosion, the desired outcome was unmistakable—bring the crew home alive. Mission Control broke the work into defined problems, and specific teams took ownership for solutions that had to work with what the crew already had onboard. One visible example was the carbon dioxide problem: flight controllers and engineers developed an improvised workaround using materials available in the spacecraft, then got clear instructions to the crew so it could be executed reliably (NASA History Office, 2011).

What made that possible was not loud leadership. It was clear leadership. A shared outcome. Visible owners. A disciplined rhythm of updates. And a system where constraints and risks surfaced early, not late. That is what steadies a canoe in dangerous water.

Let me wink back to that earlier story, the lateral move, the big shift I thought I was leading, and then the new person who arrived with no clear scope until it became obvious he had been positioned to lead the work instead.

What made that situation destabilizing was not only the decision. It was that ownership was never made visible.

I was operating like the owner. I was planning, coordinating, and trying to drive the shift forward. Meanwhile, someone else was quietly being positioned as the owner, without an upfront conversation about lanes, scope, and how the work would be divided. That is how duplication happens. That is how hesitation grows. That is how teams lose speed and start second guessing, not just the leader, but the whole system.

Here is what would have steadied the canoe. One sentence of outcome, what we were delivering, by when, and what "excellent" meant for that season. One sentence of ownership, who owns the result, who supports, and where the lanes begin and end. And one simple signal, how we will update progress and surface risks. Even if I felt disappointed, I would not have been confused. And the team would not have wasted energy reading between the lines.

Systems That Make Ownership Visible, Even Under Pressure

You do not stabilize a canoe with a speech. You stabilize it with repeatable structure and systems that ensure the consistent result you are looking for.

That is why high-stakes environments rely on clear roles and simple forms. A useful case study is the Incident Command System used in emergency response. ICS is designed for fast changing situations, and it still insists on clear assignments, unity of command, and a shared operating structure so coordination does not collapse under pressure (An Introduction to the National Incident Management System, 2020).

Even more practical, FEMA ICS forms make ownership visible on paper, not in somebody's head, such as the ICS 204 Assignment List (An Introduction to the National Incident Management System, 2020). The point is not bureaucracy. The point is steadiness. When the water gets rough, you do not want to debate who owns what. You want to return to the agreed structure.

A second recognizable example comes from Toyota's product development approach, where a single "chief engineer" role has historically been used to integrate and own the vehicle program outcome across functions, so the organization does not rely on coordination by committee (Dehoff and Loehr, 2007).

As a leader of your team, what systems are you closely creating and monitoring for sustained excellence?

If you want ownership to stay clear when pressure rises, you cannot rely on memory or "everyone knows." You need simple systems that make ownership visible, keep the canoe steady, and reduce rework. Here are the most common ones, with a real-world example under each so you can quickly spot what to copy on your team.

1. Outcome system: Define "done" in plain language

   Tactical example: At the start of a project, the owner writes a two sentence "Done Definition" at the top of the working document or project ticket:
   - What we are delivering.
   - How we will know it is done.

   Then every meeting starts with: "Has the done definition changed?" If it has, it gets rewritten in real time. No silent drift.

2. Ownership system: One owner named for every deliverable

   Tactical example: Your weekly priorities list has an "Owner" column that cannot be blank. If two people think they own it, you do not debate it in the hallway. You decide in the meeting. One owner, named out loud, with support roles clearly stated.

3. Handoff system: Standard handoff note

   Tactical example: Any handoff between people or teams requires a 60 second written handoff using the same format every time:
   - What is complete.
   - What is still open.
   - Top two risks.
   - Next step and date.

   This stops the "I thought you had that" wobble that kills speed.

4. Update system: A cadence people can count on

   Tactical example: Every owner posts a Friday update in the same place using three lines only:
   - Green, yellow, or red.
   - What changed this week.
   - What I need next and from whom.

   That one habit eliminates random pings and reduces anxiety driven rework.

5. Risk surfacing system: Make early warning normal

   Tactical example: In every meeting, you do a 90 second "wobble round" before closing:
   - What could tip us next week.
   - What is unclear.
   - Where we need help.

   This is how you get risks early, instead of surprise fires late.

6. Dependency system: Name "who we are waiting on"

   Tactical example: The team keeps a short "Waiting On" list visible in the same project space. Each item has:
   - The dependency.
   - The owner outside the team.
   - The date you will follow up.

If it hits the follow-up date twice, it automatically escalates. No quiet stalling.

7. Rework system: Debrief in 10 minutes, not 10 emails

   Tactical example: After a deliverable ships, the owner runs a 10 minute debrief with three questions:

   - What should we repeat.
   - What should we stop.
   - What should we adjust next time.

   Then the owner posts the three answers where the work lives so the learning is captured, not lost.

A Fast Leader Test

If you are seeing duplication, drift, delay, diffusion, or drain, do not ask the team to paddle harder. Pick one system above and tighten it this week. Systems make ownership repeatable. And repeatable ownership is what sustains excellence under pressure.

Paddle: Ownership Clarity Check

Use this Paddle at the start of a project, at the first sign of drift, or any time you hear the same question twice.

1. Outcome

   What are we delivering, in one sentence, and how will we know it is done?

2. Owner

   Who owns the outcome, one name?

3. Lanes

   What is included in the owner's lane, and what is explicitly outside of it?

4. Support

   Who do we need to support this, and what do we need from them, by when?

5. Signals

   What is the first visible proof of progress, and when will we see it?

   What is our update rhythm, and where will updates live?

6. Constraints

   What are the top two dependencies that could block us, and who is coordinating each one?

7. Escalation

   If we hit a wobble, who do we escalate to, and what does "fast" mean in this situation?

Part B Ownership agreement, plain language

1. Owner statement

   "I own the outcome. I will make progress visible, name risks early, ask for what I need in time, and close the loop so nobody is guessing."

2. Team statement

   "We will support the owner, raise risks early, and avoid parallel work unless we align first."

3. Leader statement

   "I will protect focus, remove blockers, and make sure ownership stays real, not symbolic."

Clear roles steady the canoe, but even when ownership is defined, teams still wobble if no one knows who gets to make the call. In Chapter 8, we move into decision rights, who decides what, when, so the team can stop stalling, second guessing, and revisiting the same issues over and over again.

Back to the Canoe

When ownership is clear, the canoe feels lighter, even if the work is heavy. When ownership is missing, the canoe feels heavier, even if everyone is paddling, because the wobble comes from uncertainty, not from clarity.

CHAPTER

8

Decision Rights: Who Decides What, When

Ownership keeps the canoe moving. Decision rights keep the canoe from stalling, swerving, or ricocheting off course.

In Chapter 7, we focused on ownership, who is accountable for the outcome, end to end. In this chapter, we build on that foundation by clarifying decision rights, who has the authority to make which calls, without waiting, reworking, or second guessing.

When teams get ownership and decision rights aligned, work moves with confidence. When they are confused or mismatched, the canoe wobbles, even if everyone is paddling hard.

Ownership and Decision Rights: Why the Difference Matters

Ownership is accountability for the outcome. It answers the question: Who makes sure this gets delivered, end to end, at the level of quality we agreed on? Decision rights are authority to decide. They answer the question: Who can make the call, approve the tradeoff, or choose the direction, without waiting for permission?

Here is why the distinction matters. Ownership without decision rights creates delay and frustration. The owner is responsible, but must constantly wait for approval, so momentum stalls. Decision rights without ownership creates diffusion. Decisions get made, but no one is accountable for execution, follow-through, or closing the loop. In canoe terms, ownership is who keeps the canoe moving toward the shoreline. Decision rights are who can change course when the water shifts.

This chapter focuses on decision rights. Ownership remains the anchor beneath it.

The Two Failure Modes When Decision Rights Are Unclear

When decision rights are not made visible, teams tend to fall into one of two predictable patterns.

Bottleneck Mode

Everything routes to one leader.

- Decisions slow down
- Work piles up
- People stop taking initiative
- The leader becomes exhausted
- The canoe stalls mid-current

Ricochet Mode

Decisions get made, then quietly revised or reversed.

- Work is undone or reworked
- People lose confidence in direction
- Trust drops because the shoreline keeps moving
- The canoe zigzags instead of advancing

A Real-World Example: Ownership Without Decision Rights

This pattern shows up often in matrixed organizations.

A program manager is named "owner" of a major initiative. She is accountable for delivery, timeline, and results. But key decisions, budget tradeoffs, staffing choices, and scope changes all require approvals from multiple senior leaders who are not in the day-to-day work.

The impact is predictable:

- Decisions stall while approvals are sought
- The owner absorbs frustration but cannot resolve it
- Teams hesitate because authority is unclear
- Speed drops
- Accountability becomes symbolic instead of real

The canoe does not stop moving entirely, but it drifts and stalls at the worst possible moments.

I have referenced that leadership wobble already, the one where I was acting like the owner of a major shift while the real authority stayed vague. I will spare you the details again. What matters here is what it did to the team: it created parallel effort, quiet second guessing, and slower execution, not because anyone was unwilling, but because no one could confidently say, "This is the lane, and this is the call." That is the damage of unclear authority. It does not just cost time. It makes people stop trusting the system enough to move with confidence, which affects performance. It also lacks the type of empowerment I mentioned in Chapter 7.

The Decision Rights Ladder: A Simple Frame

A practical way to clarify decision rights is to assign one level per decision like in the following decision rights ladder.

Decision Rights Level	What It Means	What the Team Can Expect
Decide	You make the call	We move forward after you decide
Recommend	You propose, someone else decides	You bring options and tradeoffs
Consult	You must be asked first	Your input is required
Inform	You are told after	You are kept in the loop
Execute	You carry it out	You own implementation

This is not about control. It is about speed with trust. Use this ladder as a shared language tool, not a leadership label. The goal is not to announce "who has power." The goal is to remove guessing so the work can move. Start by naming the handful of decisions that will make or break the work in this season, then assign one level per decision. When you do that, two things happen immediately. First, people stop waiting in meetings for someone to read the room and magically decide. Second, you prevent the most common trust leak on teams, the ricochet decision, where people think something is settled, then discover later it was only a draft, a suggestion, or a side conversation. The ladder helps you set expectations in advance: when you are in Decide, we move. When you are in Recommend, you bring options and tradeoffs, but you are not carrying the final call. When you are in Consult, your voice is required before we lock it in. When you are in Inform, you are not being sidelined, you are being kept aligned. And when you are in Execute, the team can count on follow-through, updates, and a closed loop. In canoe terms, the ladder tells the crew who is calling the stroke on this stretch of water so everyone can paddle in rhythm, instead of burning energy bracing for a surprise turn.

Apollo 13 remains one of the clearest examples of aligned ownership and decision rights under pressure.

After the explosion, Mission Control had to solve problems the spacecraft was never designed for: carbon dioxide removal, power management, navigation alignment, and safe reentry. What made success possible was not heroics. It was clarity.

- Outcomes were unmistakable: bring the crew home alive
- Ownership was explicit: specific teams owned defined problems
- Decision authority was clear: teams knew which calls they could make and when to escalate
- Signals were disciplined: constraints and risks surfaced early

Because decision rights were visible, teams moved fast without chaos. The canoe did not wobble, even in dangerous water.

When AI Is on the Team, Decision Boundaries Matter More

This is a forgone conclusion: AI is here to stay, and it is already a member of the team, whether anyone likes it or not. As a leader, you must put your team in the best place to accept the role it will play in driving excellence in your team's outcomes.

In our 2025 Employee Fanatix Team Culture Survey (see the Appendix), people who believed AI could help reduce burnout reported lower exhaustion. That finding is worth repeating here because it comes with a condition. Relief only shows up when leaders set clear decision boundaries so the team knows what AI can draft, what it can recommend, and where a human must decide, review, and protect trust. Without those guardrails, AI may speed up output, but it can also multiply volume and uncertainty, which creates more wobble, not less.

AI can help a team stay steady by taking some of the busywork off our plates, getting a first draft on the page faster, and making handoffs cleaner. But it can also make the canoe wobble when nobody is clearly responsible for reviewing what it produces, approval is left vague, and the team starts generating more and more output without clear standards for quality.

AI can accelerate the work, but it cannot own the work. Decision rights still have to stay human. That is one of the simplest ways to build an unshakable team and protect excellence from every angle.

AI Decision Boundary Checklist

AI can help us move faster, but it cannot replace our judgment, our relationships, or our responsibility to each other. So, we are going to be clear about how we use it. Here is our simple boundary: AI can support the work, but a human owns the work.

Ask the following questions anytime AI touches high trust or high impact work:

- What can AI draft for us?
- What can AI suggest or help us think through?
- What will AI never decide or approve?
- Who is responsible for reviewing it every time?
- If AI gets it wrong, how will we catch it quickly and fix it clearly?

This protects speed without eroding trust. When AI joins the canoe, guardrails are not about control, they are about care. They protect the human side of the work by making it clear what still requires judgment, relationship awareness, and accountability. They also calm the room, because people stop guessing what is allowed, what is trusted, and what needs a second set of eyes. Without those boundaries, AI can quietly create more noise, more drafts, more options, and more second guessing. With boundaries, AI actually does what we hoped it would do in the first place: lighten the load, reduce busywork, and free us up to do the most important part, the human part. This is the same "useful signal" idea we talked about earlier. When the team knows the rules of the water, they stop wobbling and start paddling.

I've watched healthy teams treat AI like a strong assistant, not a decision maker. They let it draft, summarize, and propose options, but they always keep a human owner for the final call and for anything that impacts trust, people, or customers. That one move alone makes AI feel supportive instead of unsettling.

Use the Paddle below to keep this front and center as you and your team navigate the rough waters that change can sometimes be. In the next chapter, I will dive into what is required to keep your team operating in rhythm as you set out on the day-to-day venture of work.

Paddle: Decision Rights Map

List the top five decisions that will determine success this season.

For each, assign one level and one name. I have added one example to the map below to make it easier to see how you can use it for your team as well.

Decision	Decide	Recommend	Consult	Inform	Execute
When a new urgent priority comes in what are we pausing, removing, or delaying?	Team leader	Direct manager, or Project lead	Upstream and downstream handoff partners	Whole team	Named owner
Decision 2					
Decision 3					
Decision 4					
Decision 5					

So, for each decision, you only answer five questions:

1. Who decides (final call)?
2. Who does the work (executes)?
3. Who must be asked first (consult needed)?
4. Who should be asked next (recommended)?
5. Who just needs to know (informed after)?

If you're ever unsure: the Decider is accountable for the call, the Executor is accountable for the result.

Clear decision rights reduce friction. They help people know when to lead, when to contribute, and when to let go. But clarity on paper does not automatically create momentum in practice. That is where operating rhythm comes in, giving the team a dependable cadence for staying aligned, protecting focus, and carrying the work forward without unnecessary drag.

Back to the Canoe

A canoe does not wobble only from effort. It wobbles when decisions stall, ricochet, or get revised in the dark. When decision rights are visible, the crew stops guessing, and the canoe moves forward with confidence.

CHAPTER

9

The Operating Rhythm: Meetings and Rituals That Protect Capacity and Focus

In Zone 1, we set the shoreline. We got clear on purpose, priorities, and the North Star values and norms, how we agree to show up while we do the work. Now we move into a truth most leaders learn the hard way: Clarity is not enough. Teams do not stay aligned because they once agreed. They stay aligned because they return to the agreement on a cadence.

That is what an operating rhythm is. It is the set of meetings, capacity-building rituals, and simple check-ins that keep the canoe steady on moving water. When the rhythm is clear, the team stops guessing, stops thrashing, and starts moving forward with confidence. When the rhythm is sloppy or overloaded, even talented teams feel like they are paddling all day and still not getting anywhere.

And here is the part I want you to remember: Meetings and rituals are where the norms get enforced. If your North Star norms live only on a slide or in a retreat workbook, they are not norms, they are hopes. The operating rhythm is where you make the norms real, one week at a time.

Fewer Meetings, Better Meetings

Most teams do not have a motivation problem; they have a focus problem. And focus gets crushed when the calendar becomes a dumping ground for every open question, every unclear decision, and every leader anxiety.

Atlassian's research with knowledge workers found that **72% say meetings are ineffective**, **78% say there are too many meetings**, and **76% say they feel drained on days filled with meetings** (Rosen et al., n.d.).

If your team feels busy but not moving, start here. Not by adding another meeting, but by auditing what your meetings are actually doing.

Here are a few signs your meetings are costing you more than they are giving you:

- People leave with more work but less clarity
- The same topics repeat because decisions are not sticking
- Meetings exist to inform, not to decide or remove blockers
- Updates dominate, but risks stay hidden until the last minute
- High performers do the real work after hours because the day was full of meetings

A meeting should do at least one of the following things. If it does not, it should not exist. Reflect on the meeting's purpose using the following list and then decide whether you are messaging, "I care about you not just for your output, but as a valued member of my team."

1. To Decide

    This meeting exists to make a clear call so the team can move forward without guessing. Deciding is an act of care because it reduces anxiety and protects people from spinning.

    Leader and team question: What decision must be made by the end of this meeting, and who will say yes or no?

2. To Align

    This meeting exists to make sure we are paddling toward the same shoreline, using the same definition of success for this season. Alignment is an act of care because it prevents rework and protects energy.

    Leader and team question: What do we need to agree on so we stop pulling in different directions?

3. To Unblock

    This meeting exists to remove friction so people can do excellent work without fighting the system. Unblocking is an act of care because it protects momentum and keeps high performers from carrying everyone else.

    Leader and team question: What is the one blocker slowing us down most, and what will we do about it today?

4. To Learn

    This meeting exists to get smarter together so we do not repeat the same pain. Learning is an act of care because it turns mistakes into progress and helps people feel safe enough to tell the truth early.

    Leader and team question: What is the lesson we need to capture now so next time is easier and better?

5. Repair Trust

    This meeting exists to clear the air when tension is rising, a miss happened, or assumptions are hardening into stories. Repair is an act of care because it protects dignity and restores the ability to work in rhythm.

Leader and team question: What needs to be named out loud so we can move forward with trust intact?

This is also where your North Star norms show up in real life. If one of your norms is "We tell the truth early," your meetings must make it safe and normal to surface risks before they become fires. If one of your norms is "We protect focus," your meetings must respect time, end with clear next steps, and stop dragging the team into unnecessary swirl. If not, you need to evaluate whether that norm is one you should keep or replace.

Here are several simple moves to make meetings more purpose-focused immediately and what it would look like in practice at a meeting.

Simple move	What it looks like in the meeting	Why it reduces wobble
Name the purpose in one sentence at the top	"Today we are here to decide X." or "Today we are solving Y."	People stop guessing why they are there.
Make the decision or problem explicit	"The decision is. . ." or "The problem we are solving is. . ."	The conversation stays on the shoreline.
Put the decision owner in the invite	Invite includes "Decision owner: Name."	The team knows who will close the loop.
Send pre-reads when the goal is alignment, not discovery	Pre-reads go out in advance with two to three focus questions.	Meeting time is used to align, not to read.
End with two lines in writing	"What we decided:" and "Who owns what by when:"	Clarity survives the meeting, even under pressure.

We have already met ICS earlier in this Zone, and it is worth bringing it back here because it models what steady teams do when the water gets rough.

In emergency response, the Incident Command System (ICS) uses short, structured touchpoints tied to an Incident Action Plan so the team is not relying on memory, personality, or who happened to be in the room. A great example is the ICS 204 Assignment List. FEMA describes the 204 as "critical for informing field staff about their assignments, duties, responsibilities" for an operational period, and notes that once the plan is approved, the Assignment Lists are included in the Incident Action Plan "for duplication and distribution

(FEMA Incident Action Planning Guide, 2012)." In other words, people leave with work that is visible, owned, and shareable, not floating around as verbal leftovers.

When the water is rough, you do not add more meetings. You tighten the rhythm, make the outputs visible, and make it easy for every paddler to know what they own next so the boat stays steady and moving.

I am like many leaders who will read this book. I spent over 20 years leading teams and sitting through countless meetings that had little purpose and even fewer intentional outcomes. I can still picture some of them, the ones I organized and the ones I just endured as a participant.

One meeting rhythm I will not forget, though, was one I did not create. I was part of a hardworking project team trying to solve a multimillion-dollar customer service problem. We were all on leaner teams, with very little time to sit in conference rooms and talk about the work instead of doing it. And yet, we started noticing something that should sound familiar. We were all busy, but the project was not actually moving forward.

That is when our project lead made a simple but brilliant shift. We moved to a decision log way of working. We named decisions, assigned clear ownership, and made sure decision rights were visible so the work could keep moving between meetings. And we only met when the meeting served one of the purpose blocks I mentioned earlier.

The impact was immediate. People felt more productive, more successful, and more aligned, because we stopped circling and started steering. We sped up milestone completion, reduced the drag, and finally brought the project to a close.

Cadence That Reduces Drag

If the previous section answered, "What is this meeting for?" This section answers, "How often do we return to what matters so we stay in rhythm?"

A steady operating rhythm is not more structure. It is the right structure. It is how a team keeps returning to the shoreline, purpose, priorities, and North Star norms, without needing a crisis to do it. Because here is the truth. Teams do not stay aligned because they once agreed. They stay aligned because they return to the agreement on a cadence.

Think of cadence like stroke rate in a canoe. Too fast and people burn out. Too slow and the canoe drifts. Just right and the team moves with less friction, with less guessing, and with far fewer "surprise" meetings that steal focus.

The goal is not to meet more. The goal is to create a few reliable touchpoints where the most important information surfaces early, while it is still small and solvable.

To meet that goal, ask "What matters most right now: What is at risk? who needs help? what decisions are coming? and what we are learning as we go?"

This is also where your North Star norms get enforced in real life. If one of your norms is "We tell the truth early," your cadence must include a predictable place where risks are raised without punishment. If one of your norms is "We protect focus," your cadence must include fewer meetings, clearer outputs, and permission to do deep work without constant interruption. Cadence is not just a calendar tool. It is a culture tool.

When cadence is unclear, teams drift into two exhausting patterns:

1. Constant interruption

   Everything becomes urgent. Meetings get added whenever anxiety spikes. Focus gets shattered.

2. Silent drift

   People stay busy, but alignment breaks quietly. Misunderstandings stack up. Risks show up late. Rework multiplies.

A clear cadence fixes both. It replaces hallway visibility with reliability. People stop guessing when they will get answers, when decisions will be made, and where to raise concerns. That reduction in guessing is a form of care. It protects capacity.

Cadence Matters Even More on Hybrid and Remote Teams

When most work happens out of view, it is easy for people to feel misaligned or isolated, even when everyone is working hard. A simple cadence gives distributed teams a shared heartbeat. It is not about surveillance. It is about steadiness. People know when clarity will be restored, and that alone lowers stress.

Here is a practical cadence that works on many teams. It is not magic, and it is not meant to make your calendar heavier. It is meant to make your team's week feel steadier. Think of it like a few reliable strokes that keep the canoe pointed in the right direction, so you are not constantly correcting course. You can adjust the timing based on your reality, but the idea stays the same. Create a small number of predictable touchpoints where clarity, ownership, and early risk sharing become normal. I have used some iteration of this over the years, and I found it kept my teams sane.

1. Weekly Focus and Alignment, 30 minutes

   This is the meeting that saves you from a week of second guessing. It is where you name what matters most, decide what can wait, and make sure the whole crew is paddling toward the same shoreline. When teams skip this, they do not become more agile. They become more fragmented.

   Purpose: Align and decide what matters most this week

   Agenda:

   - Top priorities for the week, what are we optimizing for right now
   - Decisions needed, who owns each decision, by when
   - Risks we want to surface early, before they become fires

   Leader question: What must be true by Friday for us to feel proud of this week?

   Team question: What is the one risk we should name now, while it is still small?

2. Quick Check-In, daily or three times per week, 10 minutes

This is not a status meeting. It is a steadiness meeting. It keeps little problems from becoming big ones, and it tells your team, "You do not have to carry your blockers alone." If you do this well, you will notice something powerful. People stop waiting until they are underwater to ask for help.

Purpose: Unblock and keep momentum clean

Format: Each person answers in one sentence:

- What am I moving forward today?
- What is blocking me?
- What help do I need, and from who?

Leader question: What is slowing us down that I can remove?

Team question: What do you need from me or each other to keep moving?

3. Monthly Learning Review, 45–60 minutes

This is where you protect the team from repeating the same pain. Without a learning rhythm, teams do not just move fast. They move fast into the same walls. This is also one of the best places to repair small trust misses before they harden into resentment or quiet quitting.

Purpose: Learn and repair trust when needed

Agenda:

- What went well, what should we repeat?
- What created friction, what should we stop?
- What did we learn, what do we change?
- Where did trust get stressed, what needs repair?

Leader question: What is one drag point we can remove from the system?

Team question: What is one thing we should say out loud so it does not turn into resentment?

4. Quarterly Reset, 60–90 minutes

This is your seasonal recalibration. It is where you return to the shoreline, look at the water you are in now, and decide what stays stable and what needs to change. It is also where your North Star norms stop being words and start being real. If your norm is "We protect focus," this is where you prove it by deciding what comes off the plate.

Purpose: Return to shoreline, return to norms, clarify what changes and what stays stable

Agenda:

- Shoreline check, are priorities still correct?
- Norms check, which ones are holding, which one needs strengthening?
- Role clarity check, what is fuzzy, what needs to be named?
- Capacity check, what is draining us, what do we need to protect?

Leader question: What do we need to protect so we do not burn out while we pursue excellence?

Team question: What do we need to stop doing so we can do what matters best?

That is your canoe translation. When the water gets rough, you do not add more meetings. You clarify the purpose, shorten the touchpoints, and make the outputs visible so the canoe stays steady and moving.

You might remember that hardworking project team I mentioned earlier, the one solving a multi-million-dollar customer service problem on a lean team with almost no extra time to spare. What I did not fully spell out then is why that experience matters so much here. The turning point was not a new tool or a bigger meeting cadence. It was the moment we got ruthless about purpose and follow-through. We only met when the meeting clearly fit one of the five purposes: decide, align, unblock, learn, or repair trust. And we paired that cadence with a decision log, so the work did not evaporate the moment the call ended. Decisions were captured in writing, ownership was named, and next steps had a clear "by when." That combination protected focus, cut the repeat conversations, and kept a tired team from paddling in circles. The calendar got lighter, but the execution got stronger, because clarity and ownership started living outside of people's heads. The cadence just got clearer.

Once the cadence is clear, you can feel the difference immediately. The team stops thrashing, the calendar stops being a dumping ground, and focus becomes something you can protect. Now let's make that protection real by designing the specific rituals and recovery practices that keep capacity high, especially for the people who tend to carry the most.

Rituals That Protect Focus

Meetings are events. Rituals are repeatable behaviors that shape culture. Rituals are how you keep standards stable for a season, and how you keep your North Star norms from becoming optional when pressure rises.

When a team is under pressure, the calendar fills up, the messages multiply, and people start carrying half formed decisions in their heads. That is when wobble shows up. Not because the team is lazy or uncommitted, but because clarity is living in conversations instead of living somewhere repeatable. This is where a few steady rituals can change everything. Not big, fancy process. Just simple moves that keep the canoe in rhythm so your best people are not forced to muscle the whole boat forward.

Here is a quick tip I have found useful: After a decision, capture it in writing in the simplest way possible, maybe via email. Two lines is enough. Here is what we decided. Here is why. That tiny habit stops the endless re-debating, protects the people who were not in the room, and saves your team from the quiet anxiety of wondering if the direction will change again tomorrow.

Here is another good rhythm to start if you don't do it already. Most teams do not fail because people do not work hard. They fail because work gets handed off like a hot potato. So, make handoffs simple and visible. Who owns it now. What is the next step. When is it due. Where do updates live. That is it. That one moment of clarity prevents two people from doing the same thing, or nobody doing it at all like my earlier story with me and the other new hire doing the same thing at the same time.

One final rhythm that I wish I did more as a steady cadence over my years leading teams is this: The end of week loop close. Before everyone scatters into the weekend, take five minutes to close the loop. What shipped. What moved. What is still open. What is blocking. This is not about tracking people. It is about letting the team exhale because they know what is done, what is not, and what Monday actually requires.

This is where leaders earn trust without grand speeches. People believe what you repeat. Rituals make clarity repeatable. They make focus visible. And they make the canoe steadier without requiring the team to push harder.

That is when I learned that rhythm is a form of care. Sometimes the most motivating thing you can do is remove the wobble.

Recovery Rituals: Capacity Is a Performance Strategy

I remember a season when I kept thinking my team needed more motivation, more energy, more push. But what they really needed was something much simpler and much steadier. They needed to be able to count on me.

And if I am honest, that started with something I introduced back in Zone 1, Chapter 1, steadying yourself first. Because when I was running too hard, too scattered, and too available to every meeting request, I was not actually leading. I was reacting. I was depleted. And a depleted leader is not just tired, they are unpredictable. The canoe wobbles when the person meant to steady it is getting tossed around by the current.

I was in meetings constantly. Some of them mattered, but plenty of them were just noise and I was getting pulled in every direction. Meanwhile, my team rarely saw me. They did not know if I was coming or going, if I was available or unreachable, if they should wait for me or move without me. And I could feel what that was doing to them. They were still working hard, but the energy felt off kilter. People were a little guarded. A little hesitant. Not because they did not care, but because the system around them felt unpredictable.

That was my wake-up call. They did not need a pep talk. They needed a rhythm. And they needed a leader who believed what we said earlier in the book, capacity is a performance strategy. Not a luxury. Not a soft add-on. A real requirement if you expect people to sustain excellence.

So, I made two small changes that shifted everything. First, I audited my calendar and started declining meetings I did not truly need to be in. If my presence was not essential, I stopped treating it like it was. And I did not disappear quietly, I communicated it. I let people know when I would not be in certain meetings and who could make progress without me, so the work did not stall just because my name was on an invite.

Second, when I did have to be out of pocket, I got very clear with my team about it. I would tell them, I am heading into meetings, here is when I will be back, and here is how to reach me if something urgent comes up. That one move sounds simple, but it changed the temperature in the room. Instead of guessing, they knew. Instead of scanning for me, they could focus.

And what surprised me most was how quickly the team steadied. They seemed calmer. More stable. The work flowed with less friction because access to me felt predictable again. In a way, those tweaks became a ritual. Not a formal process, just a consistent pattern that told my team, you are not alone in this canoe. You can trust when you will see me, when you can move without me, and when I will be back to help steer.

This is where the recovery conversation comes full circle. In Chapter 1, we talked about the leader steadying themselves first, not to be self-absorbed, but because your steadiness becomes the environment. And here is the next step. Once you protect your own capacity enough to lead with consistency, you can create space for your team to protect theirs too. When you do that, you send a message that lands deeper than any speech about performance. You tell them, I care about you as much as I care about what you produce.

That is a human issue. People will run hard for a leader who sees them as whole humans, not output machines. And teams will chase excellence longer, with less burnout, when recovery is not something people have to sneak, apologize for, or earn. Recovery comes in many forms. Sometimes it is reducing unnecessary meetings. Sometimes it is protecting deep work time. Sometimes it is normalizing stepping away to reset so you can come back clear. But the leadership move is the same. You make capacity visible, you protect it on purpose, and you let recovery be part of the operating rhythm, not an afterthought.

That is when the dream comes alive. Not because people are pushed harder, but because the canoe finally has a rhythm people can sustain.

And this is where Zone 1 comes full circle. In Chapter 1, we talked about steadying yourself first, because an unsteady leader creates an unsteady canoe. Here in Zone 3, the same truth applies to the whole crew. If you want sustained excellence, you must treat capacity as a performance strategy. Recovery is not softness. Recovery is what keeps the team strong enough to handle what is next.

Start with what you can control as a leader. Build in a few recovery rituals that make steadiness normal. Pick two or three from the menu below and commit to them for a season. These are leader initiated, meaning you do not have to wait for permission or perfect conditions. You can start immediately.

default pack mule. It's also a reminder that the best teams don't just work hard, they work with a rhythm, and that rhythm includes built-in moments to recalibrate communication, meetings, and expectations before the drag becomes damage.

I had a powerful recent podcast conversation with Dr. Selina Neri, Dean and Co-Founder of the Future Readiness Academy out of the United Arab Emirates. In our conversation, she names something leaders rarely get permission to say out loud—recovery is not the opposite of excellence, it is what makes excellence sustainable. I have high standards. The people around me know it. My team knows it. And still, I have learned that recovery is not a luxury, it is part of the operating system.

During our conversation, I told Selena something I believe with my whole chest, "This caring for us, this self-preservation and recovery for us, allows us to be powerhouses. I absolutely don't think I'm less excellent. I mean, anybody who's around me, who works with me on my team knows my standards are very high for them and for me."

Selena immediately took that idea and put it into language leaders can use, especially in cultures that confuse resilience with endurance. She said, "You spoke about recovery, and the resilience today has become such a buzzword that simply means in business life, go faster, hit the wall harder and keep going and pile on you more and more."

Then, she gave the reframe I want every leader to remember. She said we need to learn from sports, because elite performance has always included recovery by design, not just recovery when someone collapses. "We need to learn from the world of sports where athletes and top teams, why do they win the Olympics or the World Cup? Because they build recovery in their discipline, not just a couple of days off."

That part matters, because a couple of days off can feel like kindness, but it does not fix a broken system. Selena even said it plainly, "It's nice if my employer or my boss says, OK, Selena, great job on the project. Take a couple of days off. But that is not a long-term solution."

So, what is the long-term solution, especially for leaders responsible for results and people at the same time?

Selena calls it "regenerative resilience," and I love that phrase because it tells the truth in that it means grit and determination, yes, but with recovery in it. Then she takes it straight into leadership responsibility. Not inspiration, but systems. She said, "For an employer, this means my system of work, I need to look at where is the strain, which teams are consistently being hit and being the ones that carry the flag in the crisis while others are coasting on nice and easy waters. And I need to also understand how are people recovering from the stress or the crisis or whatever."

Read that again. That is not soft. That is operational. That is how you prevent your highest performers from quietly breaking while still producing.

Then, Selena names the real threat leaders cannot afford to ignore, "That's the only way to address a phenomenon that is the COVID of our time, which is burnout. Burnout is even more dangerous than low engagement at work."

She also said something that carries weight because it is lived experience, not just theory, "I've been in clinical burnout in my life twice. So, I know what I'm talking about."

This is why I am putting recovery in this book, because the Unshakable Team is not built by asking people to be tougher. It is built by leaders who are willing to protect capacity the same way they protect quality. **Recovery is not a reward for finishing. It is a requirement for sustaining.**

If you lead a team, here is the question Selena's words should force you to ask. Who is carrying the flag in every crisis, and what have you actually changed in the system so they can recover, not just survive?

That is the kind of leadership that keeps excellence from turning into exhaustion.

This is what steady teams do. They don't wait until people are fried to fix the system. They fix the system so people don't have to fry.

Next, we are heading into Zone 4 where I will dive into Communication and Connection, and that is exactly where teams either succeed or fail. A team that communicates and connects minimizes the wobble and learns how to sustain the stability needed to sustain excellence.

Paddle: Weekly Rhythm Planner

Use this to create a simple, repeatable operating rhythm that protects focus, makes norms real, and keeps the canoe steady.

1. North Star norms check

   Which norm are we reinforcing this week?

   Which norm tends to slip under pressure?

2. Weekly focus

   What are the top three outcomes for this week?

   What will we pause or deprioritize to protect focus?

3. Cadence

   What is our one weekly alignment meeting, day and time?

   What are our quick check-ins, how often and how long?

   Where do updates live, one place?

4. Decisions and risks

   What are the top two decisions coming this week?

   What are the top two risks, and who owns each?

5. Recovery

   What recovery ritual are we using this week?

   What is one way we will protect the pack mule problem?

By this point, you have worked on the shoreline, strengthened the crew, and stabilized the canoe itself. But even the clearest structure will not hold for long if the team has its signals crossed, if communication gets muddy, assumptions take over, and people stop feeling connected while the pressure rises. In Zone 4, we move into the steady beat that keeps a team moving forward without losing its people along the way, beginning with Chapter 10, where communication becomes the tool that calms uncertainty and reduces drag.

Back to the Canoe

A canoe does not become unshakable because everyone paddles harder. It becomes unshakable because the crew returns to what matters, on a rhythm they can count on. When your operating rhythm reinforces your North Star norms, the team stops being busy, and starts moving.

ZONE

4

The Signal: Communication and Connection

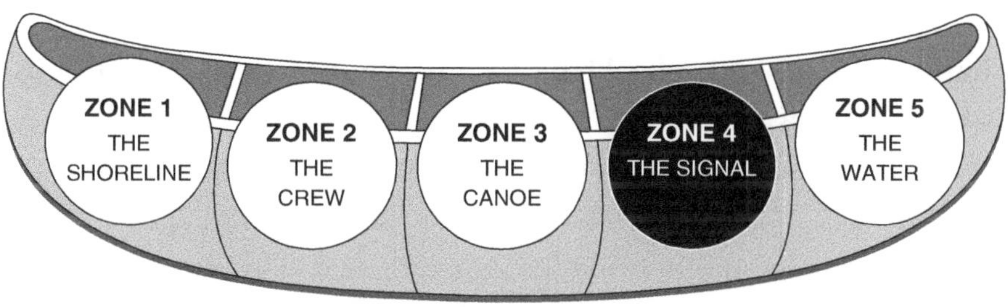

The Signal is what keeps a team moving forward without losing its people along the way. This Zone is about communication that calms uncertainty and reduces drag, and connection that keeps trust, care, and belonging alive when pressure rises.

Zone 4 is where a lot of teams either steady the canoe or slowly start taking on water without realizing it.

Because when pressure rises, most teams do not fall apart because they lack talent. They fall apart because communication gets thin, assumptions get loud, and people start paddling based on what they fear instead of what is true. That is what drag looks like in real life, rework, missed handoffs, duplicated effort, defensiveness, and a growing sense that you have to figure everything out alone. Rhythm is what prevents that. It is the steady beat that keeps clarity alive, keeps trust from quietly eroding, and keeps people connected enough to stay human while they perform.

This Zone is about making communication a stabilizer again. Not more messages, not more meetings, not more noise. Better signals. Clearer loops. A cadence your team can count on. Because when your team knows what is happening, what matters most, and what they own, they stop guessing. And when they stop guessing, they get their energy back.

Chapter 10: Communication That Reduces Drag

This is where we rebuild the basics in a way that actually works under pressure. You will learn how to replace rumor and assumption with clarity, how to set a simple communication standard the team can rely on, and how to close the loop so questions do not vanish into the void. This chapter is about reducing the friction that drains capacity, and getting the canoe moving in the same direction again.

Chapter 11: Feedback That Builds Confidence and Keeps Trust Strong

Here we make feedback feel safe enough to use and specific enough to help. Under stress, feedback often turns into either avoidance or harshness; neither one builds excellence. This chapter shows you how to give and receive feedback in a way that strengthens trust, protects dignity, and keeps performance honest without making people feel exposed.

Chapter 12: Connection That Sustains Trust Under Pressure

In this chapter we protect the human glue. Because even strong systems fail when people feel alone, unseen, or disposable. Connection is not a bonus feature; it is a performance advantage. This chapter gives you practical ways to keep care visible, keep belonging alive, and keep the crew close enough that when the water changes, they do not turn on each other, they turn toward each other.

CHAPTER

10

Communication That Reduces Drag

The Signal is what keeps a team moving forward without losing its people along the way. In the earlier Zones, we focused on the structure that steadies execution. In Zone 2, we focused on trust and care, the human foundation that makes performance sustainable.

Here is what I want you to notice. It is not an accident that I placed the "perceived softer stuff" here as well. Communication and connection are not soft. They are the system that keeps trust, care, and belonging alive once pressure rises. You can have the best plan in the world and still lose your people if your rhythm is chaotic, vague, or emotionally disconnected.

Zone 4 is where we make the human side operational. Not cheesy. Not performative. Practical.

And because every generation has lived through a different version of "work," rhythm matters even more now. Some team members want direct answers fast. Some want context so they can settle their nervous system. Some want a quick check-in to feel seen. Others want you to keep it efficient and predictable. The goal is not to communicate the same way with everyone. The goal is to communicate in a way people can count on.

In hybrid and remote work, distance creates extra drag: missed context, delayed decisions, invisible overload, and a steady drip of "Wait . . . what are we doing again?" The goal is not more meetings. The goal is clearer signals: what matters, what changed, and what happens next.

The Hidden Cost of Unclear Communication

Unclear communication does not just slow execution. It taxes trust. People start filling in the blanks with stories. And stories are heavier than facts.

I remember the one and only layoff I mentioned earlier in the book. Everyone around me was melting down. No one at the top was communicating with those in the middle and at the frontline of the organization. The whispers and assumptions took hold and only left room for the people to create their own narratives, which was very negative. I felt my own, usually upbeat self, take a mental dive around the non-communication and gossip. Change was rampant, and no one knew what would happen next and how to talk to their team members about the potential impact. Unfortunately, that company lost many of their customers and top-performing employees in the confusion.

Here are some signs that your communication is creating drag and confusion:

- The same issue resurfaces because nothing ever feels closed.
- People hesitate to move because they fear rework or reversal.
- Decisions get made, but nobody knows the "so what" for their work.

- Leaders believe they communicated, but the team still feels surprised.
- High performers quietly become the interpreters, translators, and fixers.

If you recognize any of these behaviors in your team, either directly or through their feedback, pause long enough to figure out what to do next. Do not ignore the signs, or things will get worse as the pressure is in full force. This is especially true when you take into consideration how confusing and vague communications affect the different generations on your team.

Communication and Connection Across Generations

I do not love stereotypes, because they can turn into excuses. But I do pay attention to patterns.

Some team members, often those earlier in their career, are more likely to ask, "Where do I stand?" and "What does this mean for me?" Some team members, often those who have lived through multiple corporate cycles, are more likely to ask, "What is the real plan?" and "How stable is this?"

The best leaders use signals that cover both: clarity of direction (where are we going) and clarity of impact (what it means to me). This is why communication during change isn't "extra." Gartner found that over half of HR leaders say current change communication doesn't engage employees and when people *do* have high awareness of what's happening, sustainable performance rises (Stechschulte, 2024).

That is how you reduce drag. You remove guesswork. You reduce the unnecessary nervous system load that comes with uncertainty. Here's what neuroscience makes plain: uncertainty doesn't just live in people's thoughts; it lives in their bodies. When people don't know what's coming, their nervous system stays on alert. And that "always on" feeling is exhausting. One study found that people were most stressed when the outcome was 50-50 not when pain was guaranteed and not when it was impossible. It was the not knowing that spiked stress (Grupe & Nitschke, 2013). If you want to build an unshakable team, you are in the driver's seat to make sure you are crystal clear in your communication and that you master learning to listen well.

Active Listening as a Team Operating System, Not a Soft Skill

Active listening is not a personality trait. It is a performance system. As a longtime leader of teams, I can tell you that your ability to drive excellence in outcomes is directly correlated to your ability to listen well, and not just in the way that you think.

When listening becomes a team habit, you get faster alignment because assumptions surface early. You get fewer escalations because people feel heard before they harden. You get better retention because people do not have to yell to matter. You get a better customer experience because internal friction stops leaking outward.

People most often think that communication is a one-way street, where someone tells someone something and then the other party is supposed to "get it" and all will be good. Wrong! Where most leaders and organizations fall short is in understanding that communication is a two-way street where one person communicates something verbally or non-verbally in one direction, and the other person receives what they heard or saw and then communicates something in return.

In each of my last three books, I laid out my Cycle of Active Listening™, and I am going to do that here, because I believe that if there is one lever that creates the most trust, the most buy-in, the most results, it is a leader's ability to listen well. My Cycle converts listening from a "soft skill" to the central tool used by the most excellent teams, and by extension the most excellent leaders.

Figure 10.1 shows the Cycle of Active Listening—let me walk you through each step more fully so that you can put each step to good use.

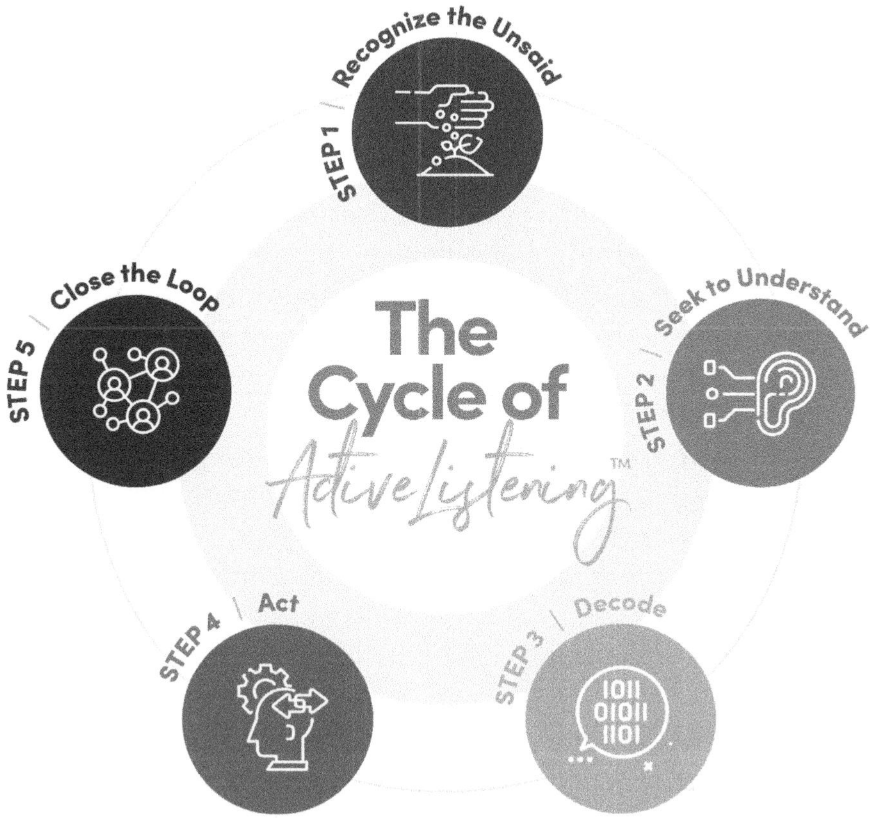

FIGURE 10.1 The Cycle of Active Listening

Step 1: Recognize the Unsaid

Pay attention to the signs, spoken or unspoken, that are right in front of you and inform what might be happening on the canoe and with your team. It's pausing long enough to recognize something is not right and needs recalibrating that allows you to move to Step 2.

Language you could use in this step:

- "I might be off, but something feels different today. What am I missing?"
- "I noticed the room got quiet. What question isn't getting asked?"

Step 2: Seek to Understand

This is the step most think of when they think of listening. You might be sitting across from a team member in a one-on-one asking them questions and shaking your head when they speak. You might even give great eye contact and repeat back what you heard. Seeking is more than this. The first question any of us should ask ourselves is this: Why am I seeking to understand this person? Is it to achieve an end for my benefit or is it to, first and foremost, help them achieve an end? In other words, are you seeking to give or are you seeking to get? We all have to answer this question before trying to give our attention to another.

Side note: If you continue to do what I said in the previous step and pause long enough to take in the entire conversation and how they feel about what they are communicating to you and you to them, you will find your seeking much more fruitful. Then, you can get to their truth for both their sake and yours.

Language you could use in this step:

- "Before we jump to solutions, what's the real worry underneath this?"
- "What would 'support' look like from me this week?"

Step 3: Decode

This is where you take everything you learned in the first two steps, and you take time to process them, reflect on them, alone or with members of your team. This pause and reflection time allows you to see if it's a macro or micro problem and decide what, if anything, you will do next. It is when the standard listen-then-immediately-act way of being changes to listen-reflect-potentially act. With this step, your team knows that you take their feedback seriously because they see that you take the time to consider next steps rather than just brushing their feedback under the rug as many leaders do.

Language you could use in this step:

- "Thank you for letting me know this. Let me sit with this before I answer. I don't want to respond fast and respond wrong."
- "What are three possible explanations for what we're seeing?"

Step 4: Act

This seems like an intuitive step: act upon what you hear. Many leaders act quickly after seeking. They think that speed of action is a caring behavior, but that is not always true. Sometimes, as leaders, you cannot act on every piece of feedback. Often it makes no sense to try. If you act too fast, you might solve for the wrong thing and make matters worse. The action needs to be strategic and well thought out.

Language you can use in this step:

- "Here's what I can do now, here's what I can't do yet, and here's what I need from you."

Step 5: Close the Loop

This step is when 95% of leaders fall. This is also the one step that has the most potent impact on building trust and psychological safety with your team, and by extension, drives more locked-in performance. This is when you go back to your team member or team members and let them know what you have done or plan to do with their feedback or requests. Most of us stop at Step 4. It's this last step that tells your team that they are important and that you respect their input. This is your #1 performance lever. Think about it: Would you fight more for excellent outcomes for a leader who makes you feel like your voice is critical to the mission, or for the leader who makes you feel like listening to you is a chore and an afterthought? Exactly. Making the choice to prioritize this step will help your team sustain excellence no matter what happens next in the environment.

Listening doesn't mean you'll say yes. It means you'll tell the truth, take people seriously, and close the loop.

Language you can use in this step.

- "Here's what changed because you spoke up."
- "Here's what didn't change, and here's why."
- "Here is what I am working on based upon your feedback."

Listening is something you *build into the way you work*, not something you hope happens when people feel brave enough to speak up. So, here are a few meeting formats that make listening normal and repeatable without turning your team into a therapy circle.

- Two-minute round: "What is the risk you want named early?"
- One sentence clarity: "Here is what I think we are solving; correct me if I am wrong."
- The leader speaks last so the team does not just mirror.

And if you're wondering, "Okay. . . how do I know this is actually working?" you won't have to guess. A listening system leaves fingerprints. You'll see it in what stops happening, what starts happening sooner, and how much less energy your team wastes trying to be heard.

Signs your listening system is working:

- Fewer "surprise escalations"
- Decisions stick more often (less re-litigating)
- People raise concerns earlier
- Less gossip/triangulation (because the direct path is safe)
- Higher follow-through (because people feel ownership)

In a recent LinkedIn poll, I asked my network: **"During major change (reorg, merger, layoffs, tech change), what's the right communication cadence from leaders?"**

Before I share what people said, let me tell you why I asked.

A few months ago, I met a senior manager on a plane who was living through a major acquisition. His team was anxious. People were scanning every calendar invite like it might contain the truth. Leaders were holding listening sessions, forming working groups, and collecting input from all angles.

At one point, he leaned over and said, **"Leadership is about making decisions and owning the result. Why do we need a committee for all this? Just make the decision!"**

Whew. That sentence stuck with me, because it captures a tension every leader faces during change: **people want clarity, leaders want speed**, and everyone is trying to keep trust intact while the ground is shifting.

Here's what I've learned after years of leading teams through change and studying and advising teams through it.

During reorgs, mergers, layoffs, and major tech shifts, the question is not, **"How much communication is enough?"**

It's **"What kind of communication builds steadiness?"**

Because too little communication creates a vacuum, and humans will fill a vacuum with fear and their own narratives.

But too much communication without decisions can create a different kind of anxiety. It feels like motion, but not progress. It can start to feel like, *"They're talking. . . but nothing is actually landing."*

So, I asked the poll because cadence is one of the fastest ways leaders either calm the nervous system of a team or accidentally spike it.

Here are the poll results:

- Weekly, consistent updates: 32%
- Twice a week brief updates: 11%
- Only when there is a decision: 8%
- Weekly updates plus decision alerts: 49%

What I love about these results is how clear the message is. Almost half of respondents (49%) want **weekly updates plus**

"decision alerts," and another 32% want **weekly, consistent updates**. Put those together and you get a strong signal: people are not asking leaders to talk nonstop. They are asking for a **steady rhythm they can count on** and then a faster pulse when something actually changes. Only 8% preferred **"only when there's a decision,"** and I get why that feels efficient to leaders. But to a team living inside uncertainty, that approach can feel like silence—and silence creates stories. The takeaway for me is simple: during major change, communication is not about volume. It's about **reliability**. Weekly updates reduce the guessing, and decision alerts reduce the rumor mill. When people know when they'll hear from you, and they trust that you'll speak up when the ground shifts, they can stop scanning every meeting invite for clues and put their energy back into doing excellent work.

If there is one place leaders lose trust during change, it is not the hard news. It is the unanswered questions that follow. In my culture work with organizations, this is the one change that I recommend the most. When we learn to close the loop in a way that leaves the team truly feeling heard, they are prepared to do what we need to sustain the excellence we are hoping for.

Close the Loop Tracker, Because Trust Dies in Unanswered Feedback

This is one of the simplest tools I know to protect trust under pressure. The purpose is not documentation. The purpose is dignity. People deserve to know their voice did not vanish.

Here are some ground rules for you to understand and live by before you even begin to use the tracker below:

- Close loops broadly when the feedback came broadly
- Close loops privately when it affects one person's dignity
- Never leave people guessing whether their voice mattered

I say this because I have worked with leaders who don't understand the ground rules of feedback. If you are operating in choppy waters and tensions are high, you want to be sure to get the basics right every time to ensure you keep everyone on the same course.

I have completed a sample tracker below to start you off in the strongest direction.

Close the Loop Tracker

What we heard	Why it matters	What we are doing or not doing	Owner	When we will update	Loop closed
That the team isn't happy about the delay in hearing about tech changes	We might not get adoption buy-in and they won't feel heard	Communicate what changes are pending and create work groups around future changes	Heather	First week in March	March 1st

This is language you can use to normalize that you want people to know that you will close the loop on their voices:

- "If you raise it, we track it."
- "If we are not doing it, we will still close the loop and tell you why."
- "Silence creates stories. This keeps us honest."

This language is important to make sure our team doesn't perceive that we have forgotten what matters to them; that we used their voices in some way.

As I think back to that day with my son's canoe story, I remember what stayed with me most. I wasn't in the canoe with him; his dad was. But I was the first person he spoke to when he got off, and his feet hit dry land. And what he shared with me wasn't just about paddling. It was about what it felt like when things got wobbly, what helped, what didn't, and how quickly your mind starts scanning for safety when you're unsure what's coming next. That's exactly what happens to people at work during change. When communication is unclear, silence fills in the blanks, and teams start bracing instead of building. But when leaders create a rhythm people can count on—and when they close the loop, so voices don't vanish, something shifts. People stop burning energy guessing. They steady. They re-engage. They give you their best again.

So, here's the next truth: communication is only half the equation. If you want a team that stays unshakable, you also need a culture where people can tell the truth early about what's working, what's wobbling, and what they need without fear. You also need a team that is open to receiving feedback that allows them to grow and become that much stronger on what might be the roughest journey ahead. That's where we're headed next. Feedback is how you keep the canoe steady mid-stream: small course corrections, real-time coaching, and honest reflection that strengthens trust instead of stressing it.

Paddle: Communication Preferences Map

Use this to reduce drag before it becomes a problem.

Ask each person, and answer it yourself, too.

1. During change, what helps you most, context, quick decisions, frequent updates, or steady reassurance?
2. What channel works best for you, live, written, short message, or detailed email?
3. How often do you want updates when things are uncertain, weekly, twice weekly, or decision alerts?
4. What makes you feel left out or blindsided?
5. What is one thing I can do as your leader that makes communication feel calmer?

Then pick one team-wide rule so everyone can count on the rhythm, for example:

Weekly update every Friday plus decision alerts within 24 hours.

If communication is the system that keeps connection alive, feedback is the practice that keeps growth alive. It helps people understand what is working, what needs attention, and how to move forward without eroding trust. In healthy teams, feedback is not a threat to belonging. It is one of the ways belonging is reinforced.

Back to the Canoe

A team can handle hard truth. What wears them down is silence with no next step.

CHAPTER

11

Feedback That Builds Confidence and Keeps Trust Strong

Feedback under stress is where a lot of leaders freeze. Not because they do not care, but because they do not want to make it worse, or they do not know what to say.

But here is the truth: silence is feedback too. And under pressure, silence usually gets interpreted as disappointment, danger, or rejection.

One of the clearest signals we have about this comes from Gallup: when employees strongly agree they have received meaningful feedback in the past week, about 7 in 10 are engaged, compared with roughly 1 in 4 when they do not (Harter, 2026).

In other words, feedback is not a "nice to have." It is one of the fastest ways to steady the canoe.

A Quick Look Back to Zone 2

In Zone 2, we talked about psychological safety as the environment, the felt sense that it is safe to speak up, admit mistakes, ask for help, and tell the truth early.

This chapter is what you do inside that environment.

If Zone 2 is the foundation, feedback is one of the daily behaviors that keeps the foundation strong. It is how you turn "safe to tell the truth" into "we actually grow from the truth." And if you want an unshakable team, you cannot make feedback an annual event. Feedback is a cadence. It is one of the most practical ways to keep a team aligned without people feeling judged.

Why Feedback Fails Under Stress

Most feedback does not fail because leaders are harsh. It fails because leaders are overwhelmed.

When pressure rises, leaders often default to what feels safest in the moment, even when it is costly over time. If you recognize any of these patterns, do not shame yourself. Just name the patterns you see. Naming the pattern is how you stop it.

Here is what tends to happen when the pressure rises:

- Leaders wait too long, so feedback feels like a surprise attack.
- What could have been a simple adjustment becomes a "big conversation." The longer you wait, the more people fill in the silence with stories.
- Feedback gets vague, so people cannot improve.
- Vague feedback sounds safer, but it leaves the person stranded. They walk away thinking, "Okay . . . but what exactly do you want me to do differently?"
- Leaders dump feedback with no support, so people feel unsafe.
- Under stress, leaders get blunt to move fast. But if the message lands without a path forward, people brace instead of build.

- People only hear feedback when something is wrong, so the team starts playing defense.
- When feedback is mostly correction, people stop taking smart risks. They aim for "not getting in trouble" instead of excellence.
- Leaders deliver feedback like a verdict instead of a path forward.
- A verdict makes people feel labeled. A path forward makes people feel coached. The same message can land completely differently depending on how you frame it.

I remember a time when I was leading customer-facing teams in a local government environment. Two team members worked closely together, and they seemed to be at odds more often than not. I found myself stepping in as the "moderator" regularly checking in, smoothing things over, and then sending them back to work.

Around that same time, I also started receiving service complaints that suggested one of them was struggling. At first, I treated the issues like they were separate: interpersonal tension over here, performance concerns over there.

Then I learned there was a deeper layer I hadn't seen in our team conversations—an inappropriate dynamic that was affecting how safe and steady one person felt at work. Nothing about it had surfaced directly in our meetings, and that was the moment I realized a leadership truth I had to own: if we only ask surface-level questions, we can miss the very thing that's quietly undermining performance, trust, and well-being.

I met with each person one-on-one to understand what was really happening. The conversations made it clear that this wasn't just a personality clash. There were boundaries that needed to be re-established, expectations that needed to be stated plainly, and support that needed to be put in place. I took the appropriate steps, involved the right internal partners, and addressed what was and wasn't acceptable.

Things improved after that. But I didn't walk away proud that I had "handled it." I walked away sobered by what I had missed early on.

Because when a leader misses the signal, the team pays twice: once in the work through mistakes, slowdowns, complaints, or confusion and once in the human cost through stress, distraction, and trust that gets strained.

That experience reinforced something I now teach: feedback and check-ins aren't only about performance correction. Sometimes they're about noticing the climate. Sometimes they're about protecting dignity and often, they're about having the courage to get curious sooner so the problem doesn't grow in the dark.

Before we talk about what to say when providing feedback, let's make feedback less intimidating by naming what kind of feedback we're giving, and why. This is not an academic model. It's my real-world way of making feedback simpler, safer, and more usable as a long-time leader of teams.

Not All Feedback Is Created Equal

Not all feedback is the same and treating it like it is creates unnecessary fear. When leaders only give feedback when something is wrong, the team starts bracing for impact every time they hear, "Can we talk?" But when you normalize different kinds of feedback, it stops feeling like judgment and starts feeling like leadership. It becomes a steady rhythm people can count on.

Here are five types of feedback excellent teams normalize, with real-world examples so you can recognize them in motion.

1: Recognition Feedback

This feedback is about reinforcing what "good" looks like so people know what to repeat. It builds confidence, strengthens standards, and quietly teaches the whole team what matters.

Real-work example:

A team member jumps in early on a risk that could have derailed a timeline. You don't just say, "thank you." You say, "I want to highlight what you did there. You named the risk early, and that protected the whole team from last-minute panic. That's the kind of ownership we're building."

This type of feedback matters, because recognition is not fluff. It is direction. It helps people keep doing the behaviors that create steadiness.

2: Coaching Feedback

This feedback is about skill-building. It's not "you messed up." It's "here's one move that will make you stronger." Coaching feedback creates growth without shame.

Real-work example:

Someone gives an update in a meeting, but it's scattered and hard to follow. Afterward you say, "You have the right information, and I want to help you land it with more power. Next time, give me the headline first, then the risk, then the ask. That will make your update easier to trust and easier to act on."

This kind of coaching feedback lowers stress because it gives people a path, not just a critique.

3: Calibration Feedback

This feedback is about alignment. It clarifies expectations before people waste energy solving the wrong problem. Calibration feedback is one of the most caring things a leader can do during change because it reduces confusion and rework.

Real-work example:

A strong performer delivers a draft that is high quality but goes far beyond what's needed. You say, "This is excellent work, and I want to protect your time. For this season, 'great' means clear and fast, not perfect and exhaustive. Let's aim for a strong 80% that we can ship, and we'll iterate from there."

Calibration feedback is important, because it keeps high performers from becoming the pack mule for standards nobody ever named.

4: Redirect Feedback

This feedback is corrective. It protects outcomes and it protects trust, because it addresses a miss without attacking the person. Redirect feedback is where leaders often freeze, but avoiding it does not preserve safety. It creates uncertainty.

Real-work example:

A team member repeatedly misses deadlines and doesn't communicate until the last minute. You say, "I want to talk about reliability. When we miss a deadline without an early heads-up, it creates scramble for others, and it damages trust in our rhythm. Going forward, I need you to flag risk as soon as you see it, not when it's already late. If you're blocked, say it early and we'll solve it together."

I know that redirect feedback feels harsh, but it is not. It's stabilizing. It keeps small issues from becoming team-wide wobble. It's caring to deliver this feedback to your team members, because without it, how will they ever learn and grow. Also, what message would you be sending the entire team if you let this type of miss go unspoken? How much more pressure will they feel to pick up the pieces?

5: Repair Feedback

This feedback is about trust and connection after friction. It's what you do when something felt off, someone got hurt, or tension is rising. Repair feedback prevents gossip and triangulation because it creates a direct path back to each other.

Real-work example:

Two colleagues clash in a meeting and the energy lingers after. You say, "I want to name something quickly. That exchange felt sharp, and I don't want it to fester into stories. What did you mean, what impact did it have, and what do we need to reset so we can work in rhythm again?"

Repair feedback is how teams stay strong under pressure. It keeps conflict from turning into culture damage. It might be hard, but top leaders know that to sustain excellence in a high-pressure environment they must be the ones to name the hard things and help everyone get back on course.

Here is the point: when teams normalize all five types, feedback stops feeling like a threat. People don't brace they learn. They don't hide they adjust. And over time, feedback becomes one of the simplest ways to keep trust strong while performance keeps rising.

Quick Glance Chart-Types of Feedback

Type of feedback	Purpose	One-line example
Recognition	Repeat what is working	"That client update was clear and calm. Do that again."
Coaching	Build skill for next time	"Next time, lead with the headline first, then the detail."
Calibration	Align on what "good" means	"For this season, good means accurate and on time, not perfect."
Redirect	Stop drift before it grows	"We cannot keep changing scope midstream. Freeze it here."
Repair	Restore trust after a miss	"I missed it. Here's what I'm changing, and by when."

Make Feedback Feel Developmental, Not Judgmental

This is where leaders often get tripped up. They think the goal is to "say it nicely." But the goal is not to be nice. The goal is to be clear and human at the same time.

The biggest shift is this: people do not fear feedback. They fear being labeled. They fear the moment where one mistake becomes a story about who they are.

So, the fastest way to reduce defensiveness is to make your intent unmistakable before you make your point. That is why I am giving you specific leader framing and team framing language here. Not so you sound scripted, but so you have steady words ready when emotion rises and you do not want to make it worse.

Let me say this here. I have had the great benefit of experiencing and delivering every type of feedback. The redirecting feedback was the hardest to take and provided me with the biggest opportunity to reflect and grow. I will never forget my very first 360 survey feedback. That is feedback where your direct reports, your manager, and other colleagues all give feedback on several fronts. As would be expected my team gave rave reviews. However, my manager had some harsh words. Honestly, he was open with the fact that he gave everyone low scores and harsh words. He told me, "You were the best of the worst." That left me flabbergasted. Was I supposed to be proud of the fact that all his direct reports scored low and I was the best of that bunch? Anyway, it took me about three months to get over the feedback. Then, I accepted what I needed to learn and moved on from there.

Looking back, that manager could have chosen his words with a more emotionally intelligent eye. That's why I want to give you some ways to frame your feedback so maybe you can provide more of a soft landing in your conversations.

Leader Framing That Lowers Defensiveness

These are phrases that communicate, "I am for you," while still being direct. They reduce the instinct to defend because they clearly signal development.

- "I am sharing this because I believe in you and I want you to win."
- "This is not a character comment. This is a performance adjustment."
- "My job is to help you get stronger, not to catch you doing something wrong."
- "Let's treat this as coaching, not court."
- "I might be missing context. Help me understand what I am not seeing."

Team Framing That Makes Feedback Normal

Now let's zoom out. The leader can do everything "right" and feedback can still feel scary if the team culture treats it like punishment. This is where your North Star norms from Zone 1 show up in real life. If your norms include truth-telling, dignity, and growth, then your feedback culture should sound like that.

You can introduce these as team agreements, repeat them out loud, and model them until they feel normal:

- "We give feedback early, not as a surprise."
- "We talk about behaviors and outcomes, not personality."
- "We assume positive intent, and we still address impact."
- "We are allowed to be learning out loud here."

These can also be made a part of the North Star norms in Zone 1 so that the shoreline becomes clearer and easier to come back to. Reflecting on the one-on-one meeting after that manager above gave me that 360 survey feedback, I was bracing for a heated meeting. I could feel my heart racing and my palms sweaty. I think I handled it well and it did not turn into a yelling match, but it would have been nice to have the right language all in my head before entering the feedback session. I want to provide some of that below.

How to Receive Feedback Without Shutting Down

Even people who want feedback can feel their nervous system tighten when they get it. That is human. So, part of building an unshakable team is giving people language they can borrow when they feel defensive or flooded.

These short responses buy time, lower emotion, and keep the conversation productive:

- "Thank you. Can you tell me one example so I can understand it clearly?"
- "What does 'better' look like in this season?"

- "What would you like me to do differently next time?"
- "Let me repeat what I heard to make sure I got it."

Now, most of above was about delivering feedback to your own team members, but I have always been impressed with leaders who accept feedback, not just from their superiors, but from those who report to them.

Feedback Is Also a Leader Practice

Here is the part many leaders avoid: if you want your team to be open, you have to go first.

When leaders do not invite reverse feedback, two things tend to happen. People either stay quiet and disengage, or they vent sideways and trust erodes. Most leaders are not afraid of feedback. They are afraid of what it will say about them.

But openness is not weakness. It is steadiness. The best leaders treat reverse feedback like navigation data. It helps you correct course before you drift too far.

That is why I am giving you multiple ways to invite reverse feedback below. You only need to pick one. The power is not in variety. The power is in consistency.

Reverse Feedback: Simple Ways to Invite It

Make it a cadence, not a dramatic moment. Pick one and repeat it until it feels normal.

1. The weekly two questions (five minutes)

   Ask in your team meeting or in writing:

   - "What is one thing I should keep doing because it is helping?"
   - "What is one thing I should adjust so we work better together?"

   This keeps feedback small and steady. It also prevents resentment from building quietly over time.

2. The monthly "make it easier" check-in:
   - "What is one part of my leadership that makes your work harder than it needs to be?"
   - Follow with: "Thank you. I am not defending. I am learning."

   This signals humility and care. It tells the team, "I want to remove friction, not add to it."
3. The decision debrief after a big call:
   - "What did I communicate clearly?"
   - "What did I leave vague?"
   - "What do you need from me next time, so we move faster with less stress?"

   This one is especially powerful because it ties feedback to speed and trust, not personality.
4. The anonymous option, if trust is still building:

   Use a simple form with three prompts:
   - "One thing we should start"
   - "One thing we should stop"
   - "One thing we should continue"

   Then close the loop out loud on what you heard and what you will do with it. Without that last step, anonymous feedback can increase cynicism, which is what I referred to in the previous chapter. Close that loop!

Leader Language That Makes Reverse Feedback Safer

Sometimes the barrier is not the process. It is fear. People are watching what happens to the first person who tells the truth. So, give them reassurance in plain language:

- "I can handle the truth. I would rather know early than pay for it later."
- "Tell me why what I just said will not work, or is not in line with our cadence?"

- "You will not be punished for honest feedback."
- "If you tell me something hard, I will thank you, not label you."
- "If I disagree, I will still respect your experience and close the loop."

At the foundation of who I am is my openness to having my mind changed by differing views, especially if the views are objectively stated and rationally outlined. I remember an early meeting with one of my new hires. She had just graduated from college a few months before, and I liked her direct nature. I let her know that I was always open to hear different opinions and that I expected her to challenge me when I might be going down the wrong road. One day, we were in a small team meeting and right after I said we should go in one direction, she said, "I don't think that makes sense." At first, my insides jumped. My inner narrative first thought, "what the heck!" Then, I remembered what I value: honesty and keeping people around me who are smarter than I am in some way. So, I took a little breath and asked her to expound of why she thought it wouldn't work. After she explained her reasoning, I agreed to adjust my position, and we went in a different direction on that project. At her mid-year performance review, I let her know that her openness to speak up and help me move in different and better directions was something I valued.

Even though we had a formal discussion about her direct nature of providing feedback, I would often just call her name in meetings and say, "What do you think about this? Is there anything I am missing here?" That cadence normalized her and the rest of the team speaking up. Inviting them to use their gifts often is the key. That is why I want to share a bit about micro feedback routines next.

Micro Feedback Routines That Build Confidence

Confidence grows when feedback is small enough to use, fast enough to matter, and clear enough to repeat. Long, heavy feedback conversations are sometimes necessary, but they should not be the only way people learn where they stand. Made it a habit to see feedback at one of your biggest performance levers no matter what is happening in the environment. Below is what a two-minute feedback loop could look like. Don't over think it and don't worry that it is short. In this case, it's not the quantity of the time, but the quality of the time.

The two-minute feedback loop:

1. Name what you saw: "Here is what I noticed. . ."
2. Name the impact: "Here is what it helped or risked. . ."
3. Name the repeat or adjust: "Do more of this" or "Tweak this one thing"
4. Close with belief: "I am telling you because I trust you with it."

This is steering, not shaming. It keeps people from drifting without making them feel attacked.

One reason I am so adamant about feedback as a rhythm is because organizations that build in frequent, human check-ins see measurable impact.

For example, Adobe replaced traditional annual performance reviews with an ongoing "Check-In" approach centered on regular expectations, feedback, and growth conversations and reported voluntary attrition decreased by 30% after the change (Doerr, 2025).

That is what happens when people are not left guessing where they stand. Clarity calms. Coaching builds. Silence erodes. And here is the quiet promise underneath all of it: when you make feedback normal, clear, and human, your team stops bracing for judgment and starts building confidence. That confidence turns into ownership. Ownership turns into follow-through, and follow-through is what keeps the canoe steady when the water gets rough. Another thing that keeps the entire team steady and ready to take on what's in front of them is the connection they feel to you and the team as a whole.

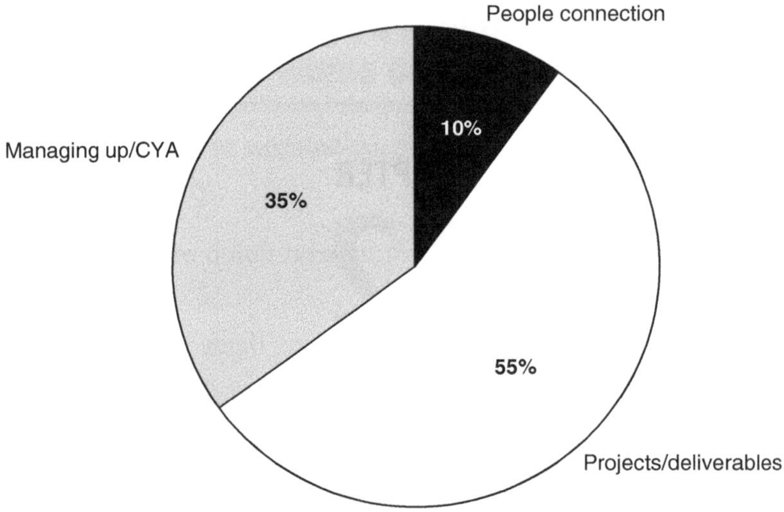

FIGURE 12.1 Leadership Prioritization Pie—Current State

Here is the truth I want to say plainly: connection is not the opposite of performance. It's one of the rhythms that makes performance sustainable.

"Connection isn't optional." It's one of the clearest signals your team uses to decide whether this canoe is safe to stay in when the water gets rough. And right now, that signal is missing more often than we think. Gallup has found that only 39% of employees strongly agree that someone at work cares about them (Harter, Workplace, 2025). When people don't feel that basic human support, they don't just feel less happy, they get quieter, more guarded, and less willing to take healthy risks for the work. If you want an unshakable team, you change the chart. You do not stop caring about results. You stop treating people connection like an optional add-on. You lean into the Ideal state shown later in this chapter.

What Connection Does in the Canoe

In canoe terms, connection is not "small talk on the boat." It's the steady hand on the shoulder that says, "*I see you. I've got you. We're still in this together.*"

When connection is strong:

- people raise concerns earlier (before they become emergencies)
- work moves with less drag (because people aren't protecting themselves from each other)
- accountability feels safer (because dignity is protected)
- change lands with less panic (because people trust the leader's intent, even when they don't love the news)

This is also why I talk about connection throughout my work, including *The Art of Caring Leadership*. Caring isn't softness. Caring is what keeps a team *steady enough* to do hard things without breaking each other.

I want to make this really practical. You don't need a retreat. You need a handful of repeatable moves you can do even on your busiest week.

Here are connection moves that don't feel forced and don't require you to change your personality.

Practical connection moves that don't feel performative

Connection move	What it sounds/looks like	Why it matters under pressure
Two-minute human check	"Before we dive in, what's one thing weighing on you this week?"	Reduces hidden stress and helps people feel seen.
Specific recognition on real work	"The way you handled ___ protected ___."	Reinforces standards and effort without fluff.
Visibility for the quiet contributor	"I want your perspective before we decide."	Prevents disengagement and surfaces insight you'd otherwise miss.
Invitation into shaping	"Do you want to be in the room where this gets built?"	Creates buy-in early before resistance hardens.
Calm truth + next step	"Here's what we know. Here's what we don't. Here's what happens next."	Replaces rumor with steadiness.

One-on-Ones: The Simplest Place Leaders Either Build Trust or Lose It

A lot of leaders treat one-on-ones like a status meeting. Under pressure, that becomes a missed opportunity. Your one-on-one is not just where you track the work. It's where you communicate, without saying it out loud:

> "You are not a cog. You're a person I'm responsible for leading and I care about you for you."

About 10 years ago, I was interviewing a job candidate with a current member of my team in the room. The candidate asked me, "Why should I choose to be on your team? What makes you different?" First off, I had never been asked that, and it was a great question. Before I could answer, my current team member jumped in to respond in a way I will never forget. He exclaimed, "It's this lady right here!" As soon as he said that, I looked around the room to see if anyone else was there. Then, I thought, "Wait! He is talking about me!" Then, I said, "Me? No!" He continued, "Yes, you. Before you became our manager, we often wouldn't even see our manager or any other leaders for months. We felt invisible in our roles. When you came along, you started scheduling team meetings and one-on-one meetings with us to see what you could do to remove barriers or ask what we needed. We finally felt noticed, valued and like a real team." Then, he looked over to the candidate and said, "She is why you should choose to come work with our team." Wow! I cannot tell you how humbling that moment was for me. I just thought I was doing my job and what you are supposed to do as a leader of teams. I didn't think I was doing anything special. This interaction made me realize how important those one-on-ones and team meetings were.

If you want an easy structure for your one-on-ones that stays human, try this:

- Start human (2 minutes): "How are you, really?"
- Then work: "What's moving? What's stuck?"

- Then future: "What support do you need from me this week?"
- Close steady: "What are we agreeing on before we leave this conversation?"

That last line matters. It's where you prevent misunderstandings. It's where you keep the canoe from wobbling in silence. An important note about one-on-ones: many leaders say they conduct these, but they often cancel and never reschedule with their team. This sends a signal that they are not important to you. They need to know they are important to you if you want them to perform at above average and at levels of excellence. Watch out for the signals you send them. Reschedule that meeting!

Connection Scales Through Small Rituals

Connection isn't only one-on-one. On great teams, connection is *built into the system.*

Researchers at the Center for Positive Organizations use the phrase "high-quality connections" to describe everyday interactions that create energy, resilience, and stronger functioning at work (Stephens, Heaphy, and Dutton, 2012). In plain language: the tiny moments add up.

Here are a few rituals that scale connection without getting cheesy:

- Two-minute round at the start of a meeting: "What's one risk you want named early?"
- Leader speaks last on important topics so people don't just mirror
- "Who are we missing?" pause before decisions to reduce blind spots
- One weekly "thank you" that ties a person's contribution to impact or standards

One of the simplest examples of connection being built into the operating system comes from The Ritz-Carlton.

Many teams know them for service, but what's interesting for *your* team is the ritual: short daily "lineups" where teams share priorities and stories of what great looks like in action, real examples, not posters on a wall (Warren, 2014).

That matters because it does two things at once:

1. It tightens standards (excellence stays visible)
2. It strengthens connection (people feel part of something shared)

In canoe language: it keeps the crew in rhythm and keeps the work human, and that is what creating an unshakable team is all about.

I want to share a moment that still stays with me, because it's such a clean example of what connection looks like when pressure is high.

I was working in an organization going through one of those seasons where it felt like we were living in constant reorgs. Not one change. A change, then another change layered on top of it. And I was hired to do a job I genuinely cared about. I had talked with my manager, Ed, many times about what I needed to move the work forward. He listened well. He tried to help. But he was also part of the broader leadership team, and there were limits to what he could fix in the moment.

Over time, I started to feel boxed in. Like I couldn't do what I was brought in to do without permissions that weren't coming. And I'll be honest, I became disheartened.

So, I did what a lot of capable leaders do when they feel stuck. I got quiet. I retreated.

I stayed close to my team on the first floor and focused on whatever we could do without needing approvals. I stopped pushing as hard for the bigger work because I didn't want to keep running into invisible walls. I didn't make noise. I didn't complain. I just . . . shrank my world to what felt possible.

And then one day, after I'd been quiet for a while, Ed showed up.

Unannounced.

He came down to my office, knocked lightly on the door frame, and stood there with this big, warm smile on his face. He said, "Can I come in?"

Of course, my first thought was, What did I do wrong?

He walked in, sat in the chair across from me, still smiling, and he didn't waste time with small talk. He said something like, "I know you feel like we've been stopping you from doing what you need to do. I know you may be feeling like you can't fully get your job done right now. And you might be feeling a little down."

And in that moment, I remember thinking: he sees it. He sees me.

Then he said, "I just want to tell you a few things. Keep your chin up. If you can be patient with us while we work through what we're working through with this reorg . . . please know you're doing a good job. We hired you for a reason. You're doing the best you can with what you've got. And we notice you. We see you."

That was it.

He smiled again, stood up, and walked out. It was a five-minute conversation.

And I can't even describe how much that moment shifted something in me. Because he didn't come to give me a new task. He didn't come to correct me. He didn't come to tell me to "hang in there" in a generic way.

He came to connect.

He met me exactly where I was with compassion and care. He picked up on the silence, and instead of punishing it or ignoring it, he got curious. He checked on me as a human being living through a hard season, and he reminded me I mattered.

To be honest, I would have done anything for that man.

After that conversation, I felt steadier. I felt seen. I felt more energized, not because the reorg magically disappeared, but because my leader reconnected me to my own agency. I started coming out of my "nest" again. I re-engaged with my team in a different way. I got back into problem-solving mode. I stopped feeling like a victim of the moment and started feeling like someone who could own the path forward, even with constraints.

That is what connection does under pressure. It doesn't remove the hard. It helps people believe they can move through the hard together. For anyone reading this who might be thinking, "I don't have any time to do this!" Remember, it only took Ed five minutes to do this. While connection to you as their leader is critical, it is also important for your team to feel connected to a bigger mission and purpose and to the organization.

Connection to Bigger Mission and Purpose

Here's the piece leaders often miss: connection is not only *to you*. It's also connection to why the work matters and who it serves, especially when everything else feels unstable.

And yes, this drives performance.

Gallup found that only 4 in 10 US employees strongly agree with the statement: "*The mission or purpose of my company makes me feel my job is important.*" Gallup also reports that moving that ratio to 8 in 10 is associated with 41% lower absenteeism, 50% fewer safety incidents, and a 33% improvement in quality (Efron, 2022).

Those numbers matter because they describe what you want in an unshakable team: fewer avoidable errors, less drifting, more consistency, and more pride in their work.

When the pressure rises through reorgs, new leaders, tighter budgets, a wave of "urgent" priorities mission connection is usually the first thing to quietly disappear. Not because leaders stop caring, but because the calendar gets loud. People start asking:

- "Does my work still matter?"
- "Are we still doing what we said we do?"
- "Am I safe here?"
- "Is this just chaos dressed up as strategy?"

This is where leaders can accidentally turn into pure output managers, and the team starts rowing hard, but without the internal "why" that makes hard seasons sustainable.

In canoe terms, mission connection is the shoreline you keep pointing to when the water gets choppy. It's how you remind people: *"We're not just busy. We're going somewhere. And your role matters on the way there."*

When purpose is clear and repeated in human language:

- People tolerate change better (because they know what's stable).
- People take more ownership (because the work feels worth owning).
- People recover faster from setbacks (because they're not just protecting themselves—they're protecting the mission).
- People stick around longer (because meaning is sticky, even when conditions aren't perfect).

This is not about posters. It's about translation. . .helping people connect *their* work to the mission in a way that feels concrete.

Here are a few repeatable moves that do that fast:

1. Translate the mission into "who we serve" (and say it out loud weekly)

   Leader language:

   - "Here's who gets helped when we do this well."
   - "Here's what breaks for customers/clients/communities when we miss."
   - "Here's what 'excellent' protects."

   This matters because mission becomes real when it's felt, not just stated.

2. Use the "Because" sentence (a five-second purpose anchor)

   Anytime you assign work, add a because:

   - "We're doing ___ because it prevents ___."
   - "We're doing ___ because it protects ___."
   - "We're doing ___ because it helps ___."

   That one word ("because") turns a task into meaning.

3. Run a quick "lineup" ritual when the team is under load

Think of my earlier The Ritz-Carlton Hotel Company example. Their short daily lineups aren't just about service, they are an operating ritual that keeps standards and shared purpose visible. In your world, this can be weekly, not daily, and it can be simple:

Here is what a Purpose Lineup could look like, in practice (just seven minutes):

- 2 minutes: "What matters most this week?"
- 2 minutes: "One example of excellent work from last week (real, specific)."
- 2 minutes: "One risk that could knock us off course."
- 1 minute: "What does the mission require of us this week?"

Notice: this doesn't require a personality change. It requires repetition.

A Purpose Check You Can Do in One-on-Ones

If you want a single question that tells you whether mission connection is alive or fading, use this:

> "What part of your work feels most connected to why we exist—and what part feels disconnected right now?"

Then, listen for what's underneath it. The answer will tell you where drag is building and where motivation is leaking. Going back to the Leadership Prioritization-Current State pie chart from earlier in this section, I'd like to propose an edit to where you spend your time as a leader. I call it your Ideal State, shown in Figure 12.2.

If your "people connection" slice grows, mission gets louder. If it shrinks, fear gets louder.

And that's the choice you make as the leader of an Unshakable Team.

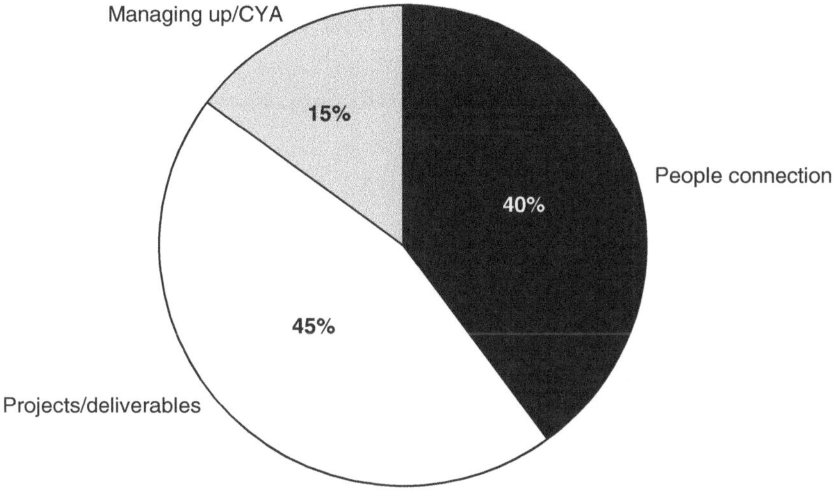

FIGURE 12.2 Leadership Prioritization Pie—Ideal State

You don't stop caring about results when you start making the connection to mission. You stop acting like purpose and people connection are optional, because the data says they're not.

When you connect people to you *and* to the mission, you don't just keep the team calm, you keep them aligned enough to perform with pride, even when the water gets rough. Connection is not something you "do" once and move on from. It's the steady tether that keeps people grounded when the pressure rises and the tasks explode. When you build it into the way you lead through small rituals, honest check-ins, meaningful recognition, and follow-through you're doing more than making people feel good. You're building the kind of trust that lets a team keep paddling when the conditions turn unpredictable. That is how you change the chart!

But even with the strongest rhythm and the healthiest connection, you can't pretend the water isn't the water. Cultures shift. Conditions change. External pressure shows up, and sometimes the biggest wobble isn't inside the canoe, it's in the current underneath it. That's why we now move into Zone 5: The Water, the reality you're leading in. You can't control every current, but you *can* learn to read conditions early, name what's happening, and adjust without capsizing.

Paddle: Connection Habit

Pick one connection habit for the next 30 days. Keep it small. Make it repeatable.

Connection habit options (pick one):

- Two-minute human check at the start of the week
- One weekly personal note tied to a real contribution
- Leader speaks last in key meetings
- "Who are we missing?" pause before decisions

Connection helps a team stay steady with each other, but even the strongest relationships will be tested when the environment itself starts to shift. In Zone 5, we move into the water, the culture and conditions around the team, and Chapter 13 begins by helping you read the early warning signs before pressure turns into panic, drift, or quiet disengagement.

Back to the Canoe

Under pressure, teams do not leave because the work is hard. They leave because they feel alone inside the work.

ZONE

5

The Water: Culture and Conditions

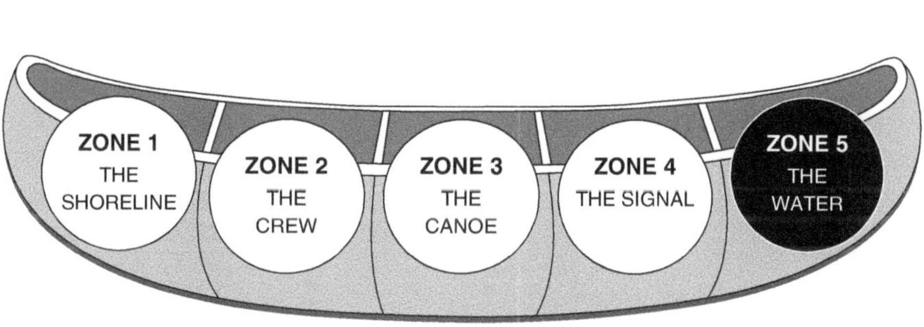

In Zone 5, you'll learn how to lead when the environment itself is shifting—pressure rising, trust wobbling, priorities changing, and tension showing up in the "undertow" of daily work. This zone is about building the kind of awareness and steadiness that keeps your team moving forward without panic, denial, or whiplash.

Chapter 13: Read the Water: Early Warning Signs and Shifting Conditions

You'll learn to spot the signals *before* performance drops or people check out—subtle shifts in energy, language, behavior, and informal networks. You'll practice naming what's changing (without catastrophizing) and responding early with clarity, care, and calm.

Chapter 14: Navigate Conflict Without Capsizing

Conflict isn't the danger; unmanaged conflict is. This chapter shows you how to stay steady in hard conversations, reduce defensiveness, and keep disagreements from turning into team fractures. You'll get practical ways to address tension directly while protecting dignity, trust, and forward motion.

Chapter 15: Change Without Whiplash

This chapter is about pacing, communication, and predictability so your team doesn't feel yanked from one urgent pivot to the next. You'll learn how to lead change with fewer surprises, cleaner expectations, and better follow-through; creating stability even when circumstances are unstable.

CHAPTER 13

Read the Water: Early Warning Signs and Shifting Conditions

Most leaders don't get surprised by a capsize. They get surprised by how long the water stayed rough while everyone acted like it was fine.

That is what this chapter is about.

In the earlier Zones, we built the canoe. We clarified the shoreline. We strengthened the crew. We tightened the systems and rhythm. Now, we talk about what leaders often underestimate: the conditions around the team are not neutral. The water changes, sometimes quickly, sometimes slowly, and your team feels it in their bodies before they can explain it with words.

And right now, the macro environment matters. People are not walking into work as blank slates. They are carrying cost of living pressure, global uncertainty, social division, constant information overload, and for many, real mental health strain. Deloitte reports that about 4 in 10 Gen Zs say they feel stressed or anxious all or most of the time (Codd, 2024).

That is not a side note. That is the water.

So, if you are leading through reorgs, layoffs, mergers, new tech, shifting strategies, new leadership, or customer chaos, you are not just managing a change plan. You are steadying nervous systems.

The Nervous System Impacts of Uncertainty at Work

Uncertainty is not only an information gap. It often gets processed as threat. When people do not know what is true, the brain tries to protect them by scanning for danger, filling in blanks, and preparing for worst-case scenarios. Research on intolerance of uncertainty and anxiety shows how uncertainty amplifies worry, hypervigilance, and distress (Grupe and Nitschke, 2013).

In plain language: when the water gets murky, people grip the paddle tighter. They become more reactive. They conserve energy. They avoid risk. They interpret silence as danger. That is why change can turn into burnout even when the workload did not technically double. The load is not only tasks. It is psychological strain.

This is also why Zone 1 matters again. Steadying yourself first is not a nice idea. It is an operational requirement. If you are dysregulated as the leader, your team will feel it. If you are steady, you can make stability louder than fear.

The Leader's Job During Change: Make Stability Louder Than Fear

And let's name what is happening underneath fear during change. Uncertainty is not just "uncomfortable." It can show up in the body like a threat signal. When people do not know what is true, the nervous system does what it was designed to do: it scans for danger, fills in missing information, and prepares for loss. That is not people being dramatic. That is biology doing its job.

Research backs up what you have probably seen in real life: uncertainty itself can drive a measurable stress response. In a Nature Communications study, researchers found that how people compute uncertainty helps explain acute stress responses, with uncertainty shaping arousal and stress reactions (Urai, Braun, and Donner, 2017). When the future feels unclear, the brain looks for certainty anywhere it can find it, including rumors, worst-case assumptions, and constant "checking for updates." That is why teams can become busy, reactive, and emotionally exhausted even when nothing has officially changed yet.

So, the leadership job during change is not just to inform. It is to reduce unnecessary threat and increase groundedness. During major change, people do not only need information. They need something steady to hold onto.

You cannot promise outcomes you do not control, but you can promise clarity, dignity, and follow-through.

Here is a simple script I love because it calms the swirl without pretending you have all the answers.

"Here's what we know right now."

"Here's what we don't know yet."

"Here's what will stay true about how we lead and communicate while we figure it out."

That last line is where your values and North Star norms stop being a slide and start being an anchor. People can tolerate hard news better than they can tolerate vague leadership.

Real Problems Versus Fear-Driven Problems

Looking back at Chapter 1 and before I dive into your team's fears, I need to restate this: as the leader of your canoe, you must steady yourself first. This also means that you must evaluate whether you are leading from a place of fear while you are leading your team. If you are, your team will take that fear on, as mentioned earlier on about emotional contagion. If you are not operating from a place of reason, but instead from emotion, your ability to meet your team with objectivity and steadiness diminishes. Utilize for yourself what I lay out below regarding spotting whether fear or reason are driving your team's response to change.

Leaders get stuck here because fear can sound like a "problem list." The key is to gently sort what you're hearing into two buckets: signal and surge.

Signal sounds like this: specific, observable, time-bound.

You'll hear things like, "Customers are asking X." "This system is breaking." "We have a deadline risk." "Three people resigned on this team." That is data. Treat it with respect.

Surge sounds like this: vague, global, catastrophic, repetitive.

You'll hear things like, "No one is safe." "They're definitely cutting us." "Nothing matters." "Why even try?" That is fear talking. Treat it with compassion, not compliance.

A simple way to do this in the moment is to ask two grounding questions:

- What do we know is true right now, and what are we assuming?
- What is within our control this week, and what is not?

Those questions do not dismiss emotion. They give emotion a container, so the team can breathe and think again. It also calms the nervous system and helps you and the team think more objectively about what is in front of you.

I still remember that feeling in my gut just a few days before I found out, with hundreds of others, that I was being laid off. I could barely sleep, but I knew something was coming. My nervous system was off the rails, and no one offered any updates or positive words to reassure me. When I got the call, I was sitting at my desk in the office, and a few others knew before I knew for sure. I remember joining a call with HR and my senior manager where they broke the news, and my head was swimming with "what am I going to do" thoughts. Over 10 years has passed since that happened, and I still wish I did not have to feel so alone, anxious, and lost through the process.

There are some practices that I have discovered over the years of leading teams through the types of change you are facing. Below are a few ways to reduce fear without overpromising:

1. Give people "small certainty" when you cannot give big certainty

    Fear spikes when people feel trapped in ambiguity. You cannot always clarify the outcome, but you can clarify the process. Tell them when the next update is coming, where questions go, how decisions will be communicated, and what will not happen without warning. Predictability is calming.

2. Convert helplessness into agency

    One of the fastest ways to lower fear is to give people a lane. Ask: "What can we control this week that keeps us strong?" Then name it in plain terms: serve customers well, protect quality, document decisions, cross-train, clean up handoffs, keep the team connected. This is not busywork. It is stabilizing the canoe. This is what I chose to do with creating that employee engagement council during the layoff. I chose to steady myself and control and influence what I could in the moment.

3. Interrupt "story spirals" with shared language

    When fear is driving the room, people don't need you to argue them out of it. They need you to name what's happening kindly. Try:

    "I hear the worry under that question."

    "Let's separate facts from the stories we are telling ourselves."

    "If we don't know yet, I won't guess. But I will tell you what I can commit to."

4. Watch for fear behaviors, not just fear words

    Fear doesn't only show up as anxiety. It shows up as:

    - over-meeting and over-checking, because people are trying to feel safe
    - delay and perfectionism, because people don't want to be blamed

- defensiveness and CYA language, because people are protecting themselves
- silence, because people stop believing it is safe to ask

When you see those patterns, don't shame them. Treat them like weather. "The water is getting choppy. Let's steady the rhythm."

A Real-World Example: Leading Through Change When You Can't Share Much Yet

I recently heard from a leader living through a company acquisition. Her message stopped me in my tracks because it names a reality a lot of leaders face, but few talk about honestly:

> Sometimes you *want* to communicate more . . . and you legally can't.

When regulatory processes are in motion, leadership can be restricted from sharing details, even when employees are anxious and desperate for clarity. But here's what doesn't pause just because the leaders can't speak freely: questions, uncertainty, rumor, and the fear that people might leave before the dust settles. This is what makes the conditions unsettling.

What this leader described is a simple but powerful shift: when you can't provide *answers*, you can still provide *steadiness*.

Instead of pretending they had more information than they did, their organization focused on building a system that made employees feel heard, respected, and kept in the loop without speculation. They created a dedicated place for employees to submit questions and a central hub where those questions could be acknowledged and answered as soon as credible information became available. Just as importantly, they kept repeating the same promise:

> "As soon as we know, you'll know."

This harkens back to my Cycle of Active Listening during high-pressure change. Your communication doesn't need to be loud, but it does need to calm the nerves of your team.

They also established a consistent cadence for live updates through regular town-hall style calls. Even when there wasn't much new to share, the consistency itself reduced panic. It told employees: "You are not being left alone in the dark."

That's what steadiness looks like when certainty isn't available yet.

During major change, people don't only need information. They need proof that leadership is paying attention. A question-hub plus a predictable update rhythm does three critical things:

- It reduces rumor by giving uncertainty a designated home.
- It lowers anxiety by replacing silence with a reliable cadence.
- It protects trust because the organization refuses to fill gaps with speculation.

And here's the subtle leadership maturity in all of it: transparency doesn't mean saying everything. It means saying what's true, saying what you can, and refusing to manufacture confidence you don't have.

If you're leading through a merger, acquisition, technology transformation, or regulatory window where communication is limited, use this as your steadiness checklist. It is inspired by the LinkedIn poll response and my own lived experience as a leader of teams and a director-level leader growing up in these environments:

1. Build a "Questions Have a Home" system

   Give people one clear place to ask. Then, make it visible that questions are being tracked.

   Leader language:
   - "If you raise it, we track it."
   - "If we don't know yet, we'll still tell you what we *do* know."
   - "We won't speculate, but we won't disappear either."

2. Separate "updates" from "decisions"

   People can handle "no decision yet" better than they can handle silence.

   Weekly or bi-weekly update structure:

   - What we know right now
   - What we still don't know
   - What's been asked most often
   - What we can promise about how we'll communicate and treat people

3. Create "decision alerts" for the moments that matter

   When something meaningful becomes true, don't wait for the next town hall.

   One simple rule:

   If it affects jobs, reporting lines, location, pay/benefits, or timelines, it gets a fast alert.

4. Reduce unnecessary interpretation work for employees

   In uncertain seasons, people become full-time detectives. That drains performance fast.

   Give them anchors:

   - "Here are the dates we can commit to reviewing again."
   - "Here's what will not change in the next X weeks."
   - "Here's what we're protecting while this unfolds (dignity, fairness, clarity, follow-through)."

5. Make managers your "calm translators"

   Employees often trust their direct leader more than corporate updates. If you are one of the most senior leaders in the organization or in your division, give managers:

   - a short weekly talking points doc
   - a "what to say when you don't know" script
   - permission to acknowledge emotion without adding speculation

Here is a quick "I don't know" manager script:

"I don't have new answers yet. I *do* have a commitment: I will not leave you guessing alone. If you're worried, tell me what you're worried about, and I'll make sure it gets raised."

Leading Indicators of Burnout and Breakdown

Burnout rarely shows up as one dramatic moment. It shows up as signals that the system is straining, the crew is compensating, and the water is changing.

I want you to watch for patterns that tell you the conditions are shifting before the team pays for it in trust, quality, or exits.

First, pay attention to the sound of the team. More whisper networks. More repeated questions. More "Did you hear. . ." and less direct truth in the room. That is not gossip as a character flaw. That is uncertainty trying to find an outlet.

Second, pay attention to the pace. When people are overloaded, they often look busy and still feel behind. Handoffs get sloppy. Small misses become normal. The work starts to wobble, and your high performers might start to hold the whole canoe steady.

Third, pay attention to energy. Not just morale, but capacity. If your team's patience is thinner, empathy is lower, and everything feels heavier than it should, don't chalk it up to attitude. That is often depletion talking.

Fourth, pay attention to you. If you feel like you are spending more time managing emotion than leading work, if you are rescuing constantly, or if you are avoiding hard conversations because you are tired, those are leader indicators the water is changing, too.

Below is an early warning dashboard. Use this when you sense something is off, but you cannot quite name it yet. Read it like a weather report. You are not trying to blame anyone. You are trying to adjust early.

Early Warning Dashboard

What's shifting	What it looks like on the team	What it looks like in individuals	What it looks like in you as the leader	The hidden cost if you ignore it
Uncertainty is rising	More rumors, more side conversations, more second guessing	More anxiety, more "just tell me what's happening"	Pressure to overexplain or go silent	Trust drops and fear fills the gaps
Psychological safety is thinning	People stop challenging ideas in the room	Nodding in meetings, venting later	Less truth, more "fine"	Risk surfaces late, decisions get weaker
Capacity is collapsing	Deadlines slip, handoffs get sloppy, quality wobbles	Irritability, missed details, more sick days	Constant rescuing, becoming the pack mule	High performers burn out, overload becomes normal
Connection is fading	Collaboration drops, tone gets transactional	Withdrawal, cynicism, sharper reactions	You default to tasks over humans	Retention risk rises, change lands with more panic
Clarity is eroding	Same questions repeat, decisions get relitigated	Whiplash, reduced initiative	You spend days cleaning up misunderstandings	Execution slows, frustration rises, culture gets brittle

This is where you earn trust. You do not earn it by pretending things are fine. You earn it by naming conditions early, calmly, and clearly, and then adjusting the way you lead so your team is not left to interpret the water alone.

What Teams Ignore Until It Is Expensive

Here is the trap. When the water gets rough, teams go into survival mode. They focus on what is urgent, they keep their heads down, and they tell themselves they will address the "people stuff" later.

But the "people stuff" is the system.

If you wait until performance drops to address conditions, you are late. If you wait until people are quitting to address trust, you are late.

If you wait until your high performers are cynical to address workload and recognition, you are late.

The earlier signal is almost always one of these: people stop telling you the truth early, people stop asking for help early, or people stop believing that speaking up matters.

And that is the bridge to the next chapter, because the moment conditions get rough, tension rises. Small misunderstandings become bigger stories. Feedback starts landing sharper. People get defensive. Leaders get impatient. Conflict doesn't arrive because your team is "bad." It arrives because the water is pushing on everyone at once.

So, in Chapter 14, we will talk about how to navigate conflict without capsizing. Not by avoiding it, and not by bulldozing through it, but by steering it in a way that protects dignity, keeps the canoe moving, and keeps trust intact.

Paddle: Use the Early Warning Dashboard

Print out the above Early Warning Dashboard and laminate it. This is a very useful tool to keep top of mind.

Once you learn to read the water, the next challenge is knowing how to respond when the pressure in the environment starts showing up between people. In Chapter 14, we move into conflict, how to navigate tension without capsizing, so the team can face hard moments directly without letting fear, blame, or emotional reactivity take over.

Back to the Canoe

Read it early, name it early. In rough water, steadiness is not a speech. It is noticing the wobble early and adjusting before the canoe tips.

CHAPTER 14

Navigate Conflict Without Capsizing

There's a version of conflict that's healthy. It's just two smart humans seeing the water differently and trying to steer well.

Then, there's conflict when the water is full of sharks. Pressure is high, stakes feel personal, people are tired, and the environment is already loud with uncertainty. In those conditions, even small moments can turn into a current that pulls the whole canoe off course.

One reason this matters more than most leaders realize is the cost. SHRM has estimated workplace incivility costs US organizations roughly $2 billion per day in lost productivity (Mayer, 2024). That's not "hurt feelings." That's performance and capacity leaking out of the canoe.

And I want to name something else that's easy to miss. In rough water, conflict rarely stays confined to "the issue." It starts to feel like identity and threat. It starts to sound like: "Do you respect me?" "Are you safe?" "Am I going to get blamed?" "Am I going to lose something?" Leaders who treat conflict like a simple communication glitch tend to get blindsided. Leaders who understand what's happening in the body can intervene earlier and prevent a small wave from becoming a capsize.

Why Conflict Hits So Hard Under Pressure

When stress stays elevated, our brains don't operate from our best selves. Chronic stress can weaken the parts of the brain that help us regulate emotions and think flexibly, especially the prefrontal cortex (McEwen, 2017). And when we feel threatened socially, the brain can respond as if it's physical pain (Eisenberger, Liberman, and Williams, 2003).

So, if someone seems "overreactive" or "irrational," it may not be a character flaw. It may be a nervous system doing its job: protect me.

Here's a line I come back to often. People don't only bring their opinions into conflict. They bring their nervous systems.

That's also why supportive relationships are not soft, they're stabilizers. Harvard's Center on the Developing Child calls supportive relationships a buffer to the stress response (Center for the Developing Child, n.d.). In grown-up work terms, connection and care help people stay regulated enough to solve real problems. I spoke about that quite a bit in Zone 4.

There's another layer here that leaders have to be honest about. Sometimes the "sharks" are not inside the canoe. They're in the water. If the broader organizational environment feels unpredictable, political, punitive, or fear-driven, your team will feel it. It shows up as sharpness, silence, anxiety, perfectionism, and blame, not because people are weak, but because they are adapting to what they think the environment requires to survive.

That's why this chapter loops us right back to Zone 1. Steadying yourself first is imperative. If you are dysregulated as the leader, your team will feel it. If you can steady yourself first, you can settle the waters.

Uncertainty is one of the most destabilizing conditions humans can sit in for long periods of time. Our nervous systems treat "I don't know what's coming" like a threat, and threat makes us scan, brace, and protect.

So, when a leader says, "They should just wait until we know more," I get it. But biology doesn't work that way. People fill the gaps. As previously stated, when leaders don't fill the vacuum with calm truth and follow-through, fear will fill it with worst-case stories.

That does not mean you should communicate constantly or speculate. It means you should lead uncertainty on purpose. You reduce threat by increasing steadiness. You don't have to control the water to keep the canoe from flipping.

Conflict Styles Under Pressure

Most teams don't need a personality assessment to understand what's happening. You can usually spot the pattern in real time.

Some people go sharp. They push, correct, dominate, or "win." When the water feels unsafe, sharpness can feel like control. They'd rather be disliked than surprised. They may call it "high standards," but underneath it's often fear of failure, fear of being blamed, or fear of being made irrelevant.

Some people go silent. They disappear, comply, or retreat. Silence is not always agreement; a lot of times it's self-protection. They're deciding, consciously or unconsciously, "It's safer to be invisible than to be wrong." The risk is that silence turns into resentment, and resentment eventually turns into exits. Honestly, this is more my style. Remember my earlier story about Ed, my manager during those multiple reorgs? I was in pure retreat mode. I was exhausted by what I felt was a fight to be able to get my job done in the middle of those constant changes. I just interacted mostly with everyone else but the executive team so I would not have to enter into the high-tension territory.

Some people go sideways. They vent, triangulate, gather allies, and turn tension into a story. This is what happens when the direct path doesn't feel safe. Sideways communication is often an attempt to find security through community, but it creates drag fast. It pulls paddlers out of rhythm and turns the canoe into camps.

Some people go perfectionist. They overexplain, overdocument, and try to control the water through detail. Perfectionism is what it looks like when someone is trying to build certainty out of paperwork. It can sound like diligence, but the emotional driver is often: "If I can't trust the environment, I'll at least be able to prove I wasn't the problem."

None of these are "bad people." They're predictable protection moves.

Your job as the leader of your team is to interrupt the pattern before it becomes identity: "That's just how she is." "That's just how he is." No. That's how the water is affecting them.

And here is one of the smallest "steady yourself" moments that changes everything. I started to ask myself this question too through every changing environment I entered:

Ask: Am I here to be right, or am I here to repair and move us forward?

Then take a breath, lower your speed, slow your voice, and loosen your face.

As I've said elsewhere in this book, your nervous system is contagious, and you're the loudest signal in the room. If you want to be right, buckle up for a rocky ride. If you want to move forward, and maybe even from a place of peace, take a breath.

Move from Blame to Repair

Blame is what people do when they're scared and trying to locate fault so they can feel safe again. Repair is what steady leaders do to keep dignity intact and restore forward motion.

Blame says, who caused this?

Repair says, what happened, what did it impact, and what do we need to change so it doesn't happen again?

You can feel the difference in the body. Blame tightens. Repair opens. Repair is where performance comes back online. Blame shuts performance down quickly.

When I talk about the difference between blame and repair, I'm not speaking in theory. I've watched it play out in real time, and I've felt it in my own body.

I remember a moment when one of my direct reports, a manager on my team, looped me on an email exchange with one of her employees. The second I read it, I knew something was off. Her tone was curt, sharp, blame-y. And what stopped me in my tracks was this: it was completely unlike her. She wasn't a leader who normally led that way.

My immediate reaction was physical. I felt myself clench. I got a little heated. You know that sensation when your chest tightens and your brain goes, Oh no . . . this is going to get messy. For a split second, I wanted to jump in and correct it right then, right there, in the email thread.

But I didn't.

I took a breath. Not a dramatic one. Just enough to bring myself back to steady. Because I've learned the hard way: if I respond while I'm activated, I'm more likely to create more heat than help.

So instead of replying with emotion, I responded with leadership. I asked her to come into my office so we could talk.

When she came in, I started with honesty and care. I told her I was genuinely surprised by what I read, because it didn't sound like her, and then I did the most important thing a leader can do in moments like this: I got curious before I got corrective. I asked her what was going on, what the tension was really about, and what she believed had happened between her and the employee.

She explained the situation from her perspective, and I listened. Then I said something along the lines of, "this is not how you normally show up, and I need you to see that the way this landed could damage trust."

Then, I put the responsibility where it belonged. I didn't make myself the fixer. I asked her, what are you going to do to repair this?

That question matters, because blame wants punishment. Repair wants restoration.

She paused, and to her credit, she owned it. She decided to take the employee to lunch, acknowledge how her communication came across, apologize for the tone, and talk through how they could work together moving forward.

Were they best friends after that? No. But they were able to reset enough to work cordially and rebuild a functional relationship. And that's the point. Repair doesn't always mean closeness. Sometimes repair simply means we stop bleeding trust in the day-to-day.

What I took from that moment is something I want you to remember in your own leadership: you can feel the difference between blame and repair, and it shows up fast. Blame tightens the room. Repair steadies it. But moving to repair takes self-control. It takes a pause. It takes the decision to lead your nervous system first, so you don't accidentally lead with heat.

That day, the breath I took before responding wasn't small. It was the hinge. It was the moment I chose steadiness over reaction, and it gave my leader space to do the same.

When the Water Is Toxic, Protect the Canoe Anyway

Now, let's talk about the harder scenario, because some of you are leading in water that is not just choppy. It is corrosive, and I alluded to this above.

When the organizational culture feels toxic, the leader's job expands. You're not only managing conflict between people. You're also protecting your team from an environment that trains people to be defensive.

Toxic doesn't always mean dramatic. Sometimes it's death by a thousand cuts: disrespect that's tolerated, constant second guessing, unclear decision-making, public shaming, shifting expectations, fear of blame, or leaders who weaponize urgency.

Research on workplace incivility has shown that when people experience disrespect at work, they often respond in ways that quietly drain performance, like reducing effort, avoiding the offender, and losing time worrying about the incident (Porath and Pearson, 2013). That is drag. That is capacity loss. That is people paddling with one hand because the other hand is busy protecting them. Sustaining excellence becomes even more challenging in these waters.

So, what do you do if you can't fix the whole waterway?

You create a microclimate.

You may not be able to change the entire organizational culture quickly, but you can make your team's "way of being" clear and consistent. You can make respect non-negotiable. You can make direct communication safe. You can make repair normal. You can stop rewarding blame as if it's competence. That is your span of control. Do not abdicate your responsibility in this area.

This is one of the most important leadership distinctions in rough water.

Busy can be solved with structure.

Toxic requires boundaries, clarity, and courage.

Here's what I want you to hear as a leader: if you tolerate corrosive behavior, you don't just "avoid conflict." You normalize it. And once it becomes normal, your best people start asking themselves quietly, how long do I want to live in this water?

Apollo 13 is still a masterclass in this chapter because the pressure was real, the stakes were life and death, and the only way through was disciplined communication and clear roles. They didn't have the luxury of emotional spirals, but they also didn't pretend emotions weren't present. They used structure to keep fear from driving the boat.

That's a leadership lesson worth repeating. You don't eliminate emotion. You lead it.

Years ago, I was working in an organization where the CEO set the climate for the office and for the division, and the truth is, most people didn't trust him. Not because of one big scandal, but because of a pattern. The kind of habits that make people feel watched, not led.

He would skulk around the office. Peek around corners. Ask questions in passing without context. He wasn't transparent, but he expected everyone else to be. Over time, that does something to people. It doesn't just create frustration, it creates hypervigilance. People start looking over their shoulder. They stop trusting questions, because every question feels like a test. They start playing defense. They start covering themselves, and before you know it, you're not operating in a culture of truth. You're operating in a culture of fear.

What made it harder is that our expectations were still high. Customers still needed great service. Metrics still mattered, and at the same time, we were in the middle of a private equity firm purchasing the company. So yes, my nerves were high. Everyone's nerves were high. The water already had waves, and then the person at the top made the water feel shark-filled.

As a leader in that environment, I learned something that I wish no leader ever had to learn the hard way: when the culture above you is dysregulating, your job becomes being a steady nervous system on purpose.

And I had to do it in layers.

First, I had to stop victimizing myself under his leadership. I don't mean pretending it wasn't happening. I mean refusing to let his behavior become the story I lived inside all day. Because if I let myself spiral, I would be leading from the same fear I was trying to protect my team from.

Second, I had to regulate myself before I tried to regulate anyone else. I had to watch my own tone. My own speed. My own reactivity. There were days I wanted to vent with my team, because they were venting too. But I could feel the difference between connection and contamination. I didn't want to pour gasoline on their anxiety. I wanted to give them something steadier to hold onto.

Third, I had to let some of it roll off my shoulders, not because it didn't matter, but because I couldn't afford to carry it. I still had a canoe to steer. I still had people who were watching me closely, trying to figure out: Are we safe? Are we going to be okay? Can we trust what's coming next?

So, I doubled down on what I could control.

I got clearer. I communicated more directly. I reinforced our norms. I named what I did and didn't know. I made sure my team didn't have to guess where I stood, what mattered, or how we would handle pressure. I tried to make our little corner of the organization feel different than the bigger climate. Not perfect. Not immune. But steadier.

Because when the water around you is full of sharks, you don't win by pretending the sharks aren't there. You win by keeping the crew calm enough to paddle, clear enough to make good decisions, and connected enough to not turn on each other.

That season didn't magically become easy. The deal still moved forward. The uncertainty still existed. The CEO didn't suddenly become a trust-builder, but my team stayed more stable than they would have otherwise, because we had one place in the water where people weren't constantly bracing. One canoe where the leader wasn't adding fear to fear.

That's why I'm so serious about what I said earlier in this chapter. If you tolerate corrosive behavior, you normalize it. But if you interrupt it, even when you can't eliminate it, you protect your people. You keep the conflict from becoming identity. You keep fear from becoming culture.

In rough water, that is leadership.

The goal of conflict leadership is not to make the team feel nothing. It's to keep the team human enough to tell the truth, clear enough to solve the real problem, and steady enough to move forward without damaging each other.

Conflict is one of the most visible signs that the water is getting rough, but if we're honest, it's rarely the root problem. Most conflict is a symptom of speed without clarity, change without closure, and pressure without enough steadiness to hold people together. When leaders don't name the current, teams start bumping into each other inside the canoe. They protect themselves. They snap. They shut down. They turn small moments into stories. That's why the real work of conflict isn't just "handling the hard conversation." It's building a way of leading that keeps the canoe steady even when everything outside of it is shifting. Because the truth is, change is inevitable. But whiplash is optional, and in the final chapter of this Zone, we're going to talk about what it looks like to lead change without exhausting your people, without breaking trust, and without letting the team feel like they're bracing for impact every week.

Paddle: Conflict Reset Conversation

Use this when tension is high, emotions are up, or the story is getting sharper than the facts. This is not a script to win. It's a structure to keep dignity intact and get the canoe moving again.

Step 1: Name the shared shoreline so you're not fighting two battles

Leader: Before we get into the details, can we agree on what we both want to protect here?

Examples might include the customer experience, the timeline, quality, trust on the team, safety, fairness.

Step 2: Describe what you observed, not what you assume

Leader: Here's what I saw or heard.

This is where you stay away from "you always," "you don't care," "you were trying to," because assumptions light people up fast.

Step 3: Name impact in human terms

Leader: Here's what that created for me or for us.

Name what it actually caused, like drag, confusion, rework, distrust, embarrassment, missed handoffs, or people withdrawing.

Step 4: Get curious about the story underneath

Leader: What was going on for you in that moment?

Leader: What did you need that you didn't feel you had?

This is where fear often shows itself without being shamed.

Step 5: Make one clear request and one clear commitment

Leader: Here's what I need going forward.

Leader: Here's what I will do differently too.

This is how you move from "discussion" to "repair."

Step 6: Close the loop so it doesn't reopen as gossip

Leader: What did we agree to?

Leader: How will we handle it if we start drifting back into the same pattern?

If you want a deeper refresher on closing the loop, look back to Zone 4.

Leader language that de-escalates fast, use sparingly, but use it:

- "Pause. I don't want us to damage trust while we're trying to solve a real problem."
- "I might be missing context. Help me understand."
- "Let's stay on the issue, not each other."
- "We can be honest and still be kind."
- "I'm not asking you to be perfect. I'm asking you to be clear."

We are now moving away from the conflict that can sink the canoe if not mitigated proactively to making sure we focus on the tools that diagnose, stabilize, and sustain when the water gets rougher than usual. This final chapter is where we lock in on a different kind of resilience and leading in rough water.

Back to the Canoe

When conflict becomes personal, the canoe doesn't just wobble, it starts to take on water. Your job is not to eliminate hard conversations. Your job is to keep them human enough that the team can stay in the boat together and keep moving forward.

CHAPTER

15

Change Without Whiplash

Change is inevitable. Whiplash is not.

Most leaders don't struggle because they "can't handle change." They struggle because change keeps coming without rhythm, without closure, and without respect for the humans doing the work. One change lands, and before the team can stabilize, another wave hits. Priorities shift, organizational charts shift, tools shift and expectations shift. Then, people are left bracing instead of building.

In canoe terms, this is what whiplash looks like: the water keeps changing, but the crew never gets a chance to reset their stroke. They start paddling in survival mode. Some paddle harder. Some paddle quieter. Some stop paddling at all. Not because they're weak, but because the conditions never let them recover, recalibrate, or trust what "normal" even is anymore.

Here's what I want you to hear clearly as you step into this final chapter: unshakable teams don't avoid hard water. They learn how to move through it without losing themselves.

A Quick Flashback to the Canoe

I've shared the canoe story throughout this book because it captures something leaders often miss: the goal isn't to pretend the water isn't rough. The goal is to keep the boat steady enough to keep moving.

There's a moment in that story I keep coming back to. My son got off the canoe and onto dry land, and I was the first person he spoke to. What he needed in that moment wasn't a debrief on technique. He needed steadiness. He needed someone to help his nervous system come back down. He needed reassurance that he was safe, that he wasn't alone, and that the experience didn't define his future.

That's what your team needs during major change, too.

Not a motivational poster. Not "embrace the change." Not more town halls with fewer answers.

They need a leader who can say, with integrity: I can't control every current, but I can help you stay steady in this water, and we will achieve great things no matter what happens next!

Change Management Versus Change Leadership (and Why Unshakable Teams Need Both)

Let's simplify something that gets overcomplicated.

Change management is the logistics: plans, timelines, training, processes, deliverables, communication calendars, milestones.

Change leadership is the human side of the canoe. Clarity. Trust. Emotional steadiness. Decision integrity. Follow-through. Dignity. Ownership. Meaning.

A lot of organizations attempt transformation like it's purely operational, but research repeatedly shows that transformations fail far more often than leaders want to admit. McKinsey has cited that transformation efforts fail around 70% of the time (McKinsey Transformations, 2019).

That number should sober us up, because it's not that people can't change. It's that too many leaders try to move the canoe by shouting new directions while ignoring the crew's capacity, fear, and fatigue.

So, this chapter is not just "how to manage change." It's how to lead change without breaking people. Before I move forward, let's talk about the whiplash caused by the continued change initiatives that don't seem to let up.

Whiplash is what happens when any of these become normal:

- People don't know what matters most this week.
- People don't know who owns decisions.
- People don't know what's real versus rumor.
- People don't know how long the uncertainty will last.
- People don't know whether their leaders are telling them the truth.
- People don't know if their effort will matter because priorities may change again by Friday.

When your team is stuck in that state, performance doesn't just dip. People start scanning the environment for danger. They get more cautious. They get more reactive. They get more tired. They protect themselves and even the most talented teams start leaking capacity, which means that your goal of team excellence goes out the window.

This is where Zone 1 comes roaring back into the story.

Do whatever you need to do to steady yourself first. If you are anxious, exhausted, in pain, operating on empty, what do you think your team will emulate?

Remember my personal story back in Chapter 1 of Zone 1, when I was going through a second reorg in less than six months? I had just walked out of a meeting, and I was not in a good place mentally when I re-entered the area where my entire team sat.

At the time, I didn't fully understand the ripple effect of what I was carrying on my face, in my energy, and in the way I moved back into the room. I wasn't trying to send a message, but I did. The message they received wasn't, "We're going to be okay." It was, "Even she isn't sure we're going to be okay."

I didn't intend to hurt them, but I did. I dented their confidence in my ability to navigate choppy waters and, by extension, I dented their confidence in themselves to navigate those same waters with steadiness. This was an important turning point in my leadership. I realized in that moment that if I did not get ahold of my own nervous system and grow in emotional self-control, I'd only be a mediocre leader, at best. I also realized I could not expect excellence out of my team when I was broken and unable to lead them to excellent outcomes.

From "Bounce Back" to "Build What Holds"

We have taught leaders and teams that resilience is about getting knocked down and getting back up. Over and over again. And when we do that, we normalize struggle as the price of performance as if there is a "hit the wall the most" trophy!

That's why I call this work Unshakable Leadership™ and embedded in that is The Unshakable Team. It's the antidote to short-term resilience in a vacuum, because it gives leaders the layers that make steadiness repeatable.

Think of it like this: there is resilience in the moment and then there is steady by design. Let's start with the first.

1. Resilience in the Moment

This is what people usually mean by resilience. It's the ability to stay functional when the pressure spikes. It is reframing, self-talk, grounding, and simply getting through the next 24–72 hours without capsizing.

This resilience in the moment matters. Because there will be moments when the water shifts suddenly and you don't have time to redesign the canoe. You must survive the threat and help the crew survive the moment as well.

Most leaders think resilience is something you either "have" or you don't. Like grit. Like toughness. Like you just take the hit, swallow it, and keep paddling, and taking the hit has become a badge of honor.

But as I've lived this work, coached it, and studied it, I realized that resilience alone, in its current definition, is overrated. Yes, it's great to be able to bounce back from adversity, to make a good next decision while the water is still moving, but the goal shouldn't be the "bounce-back." It should be to build something that holds. To build steady, unshakable leaders, teams, and cultures under pressure.

Steady by design is what you build so your team doesn't have to rely on adrenaline and heroics to survive the season.

Both matter. And if you want an unshakable team, you need both.

I recently interviewed Amy Edmondson on my *Becoming Unshakable* podcast. Amy is a Harvard Business School professor and is widely known for her work on psychological safety (hence why I mentioned her earlier in the book). She's also written a powerful book on failure called *Right Kind of Wrong*. During our conversation, I asked her a question I think every leader is asking right now, whether they say it out loud or not:

"What's the toolkit for being unshakable?" The tool she shared was simple enough to remember under pressure, which is exactly why it matters, and why I am sharing it now. She calls it:

"Stop, Challenge, Choose."

Here's why I love it. It respects the fact that when pressure spikes, your nervous system is already doing something. You get hooked. You get activated. You get anxious. Your mind starts narrating worst-case scenarios like they're facts.

In canoe terms, this is the moment your paddle starts splashing instead of stroking. The water hasn't necessarily gotten more dangerous yet, but your body is reacting like it has.

"Stop" is the pause. The breath. The interruption.

Not a dramatic, spa-like pause. A real one. The kind you do at your desk, in the hallway, after a meeting, staring at a Slack message that just lit you up.

Stop is how you keep the moment from driving you.

"Challenge" is where you take a quick look at the story you're telling yourself.

Amy described how our thinking often goes straight to catastrophic. The brain starts sprinting: This is awful! This is going to ruin everything! I'm failing! We're failing! I can't handle this! I call this falling into a pit of despair.

Challenge doesn't deny the pressure. It just asks: Is my thinking helping me right now, or hijacking me?

Then, "Choose" is where leadership comes back online. Choose is the deliberate response. The next best step. The version of you that is steady enough to lead.

Choose sounds like: What response would be in my team's best interest right now? What would the leader I want to be do next?

Sometimes that "choose" is simple. It's opening the document and doing the hard thing you've been avoiding. It's sending the clarifying message. It's walking down the hall to have the conversation instead of letting it rot in email. Sometimes, "choose" is choosing to wait. Choosing to sleep on it. Choosing not to respond while your nervous system is hot.

This is resilience in the moment, not powering through, but regaining your steering.

If you have read this far, you will remember the story of my first and only layoff. I still remember the moment they told me. It wasn't a long conversation. It was a call, and the message was simple and sharp: I was being laid off, and I was leaving that day.

What happened in me, immediately, was not "professional." It was human.

My body reacted first. My chest tightened. My stomach dropped. My throat got that hot, thick feeling that tells you tears are coming whether you want them or not. I remember doing everything I could to hold it together in the moment, not because I wasn't hurting, but because I was trying to survive the shock without falling apart in front of the people delivering it.

Then my mind did what minds do under threat. It started telling stories.

Not thoughtful stories. Not wise stories. Fast stories.

I felt lost, I felt scared, I felt ashamed, and if I'm being honest, there was a moment where my mind wanted to go to extremes. Not in a literal sense, but in that emotional way people do when they're hooked under pressure. The part of me that felt panicked wanted to make a rash decision somewhere else, to grab control of anything I could grab. That's what "wobble" looks like from the inside. It's not always loud. Sometimes it's quiet and frantic at the same time.

I could feel myself right on the edge of reacting in a way that would have created even more instability in my life. That's when I did the first thing that helped me interrupt the spiral. I went to my church. I sat with my pastor, and I didn't pretend I was fine. I cried. I let the emotion come out. I didn't try to be strong in the way people think strength looks. I chose the kind of strength that tells the truth, and he reassured me, simply, that I was going to be okay.

That conversation didn't magically erase what happened. I still had days afterward where I felt unsteady. I still moved through doubt, fear, confusion, and that lingering question that layoffs always leave behind: What does this mean about me? That meeting did one critical thing. It calmed my nervous system enough to give me back my agency. Once I could breathe again, I made a decision that changed everything: I needed to do something I could influence.

So instead of letting the layoff write the story for me, I picked up the pen. I went online and wrote one of my very first LinkedIn articles, and the topic wasn't random. It came straight from the moment I was living through. I wrote about how to lay people off with dignity.

That article got engagement. People responded. People shared. People reached out, and what happened next surprised me: that one choice became a turning point. It set a course for me becoming active on LinkedIn, which later became a meaningful driver of my business. Clients came from there. Opportunities came from there. Momentum started to return.

More importantly, *I* started to return.

That's what resilience in the moment looked like for me. It wasn't denial. It wasn't pretending I wasn't scared. It was letting myself feel the impact, finding a steady voice to borrow until I could hear my own again, and then choosing one action that brought me back to solid ground.

The layoff created wobble in me. There's no way around that, but I didn't stay there. I interrupted the story my fear was trying to write, and I chose a different one. I chose dignity. I chose purpose. I chose movement. I chose influence, and that's the part I want you to hold onto: when life or work knocks the breath out of you, you don't have to act from the hook. You can pause long enough to steady and then choose the next right move. One move. The kind you can stand on.

In that layoff season, I needed resilience in the moment, but what I've learned since is this: the teams that thrive long-term don't rely on heroic personal grit. They rely on systems. That's why Zone 1 through Zone 5 exist. Steady by design is what happens when you build the shoreline, the crew, the canoe, the signals, and the water-reading skills so your team can stay steady even when the environment isn't. The Zones are how you do it. Let's talk about that next. . ..

2. Steady by Design

This next focus is not just on coping, but it's on constructing the conditions that make coping less necessary. It's building a team that doesn't require a badge of honor to survive. If resilience asks, "Can I recover after pressure?" Steadiness asks, "Can people trust my presence, judgment, care, and clarity while the pressure is still unfolding?"

Steady by design isn't about who can endure the most. It's about what we've built so the team doesn't have to live in endurance mode in the first place. Now, let me zoom out, because this is where most leaders miss the bigger picture.

If resilience is only something you do in the moment, you'll spend your whole leadership life in reaction mode. Believe me, I tried this. You'll keep asking people to "be resilient," when what they really need is a team system that doesn't require constant self-rescue.

This is why *The Unshakable Team* is not another resilience book. Though, it is true that resilience is embedded into the operating system.

This book is steady by design, because when the Zones are strong, the focus becomes less about the moment and more about architecting the whole. Each Zone adds the needed layer to help your team sustain into the future not just for today. It's the difference between a team that survives because they're tough, and a team that stays steady because the structure supports them.

Here's the part I want to be clear about, especially for high-performing leaders: if you only build "bounce back" resilience, you'll create a culture of endurance, but if you build steady by design, you create a culture of care and stability. That's how excellence stays sustainable.

So, here's the framework I want to introduce as we close this out. You can name it later. For now, I want you to feel the architecture of it. Because once you see it, you'll stop treating resilience like a pep talk and start treating it like leadership design.

The Steady by Design Framework: Three Levels Leaders Must Build

When most leaders think about resilience, they think about what an individual does in a hard moment. That's important, but it's only the first layer. I am calling this steady by design, because I don't think our current understanding of leading through pressure is sufficient. In my view, steady by design has three layers, and they build on each other and are adapted from modern psychology and environment ecosystem perspectives.

Level 1: Nervous System Steadiness (Me)

This is where everything begins, and it's why Zone 1 matters so much. If you remember the early chapters, you already know this isn't a "nice-to-have." It's an operational requirement.

When pressure rises, your body reacts before your mind catches up. Your face changes. Your tone changes. Your pace changes, and your team feels it. They may not be able to name it, but they can sense it instantly.

This is why steadying yourself first is the highest form of leadership. It's nervous system leadership.

At this level, steady by design looks like a leader who can slow down fast enough to choose, instead of react. A leader who can interrupt their own fear story. A leader who protects capacity, because they know capacity is a performance strategy. A leader who knows that they cannot do it all alone and so they call in help. If your nervous system is chaotic, your team will feel it before they hear it.

Level 2: Team Operating Steadiness (We)

This is where leadership becomes a shared operating system. This is Zones 2 through 4 coming alive.

It's trust and care that makes truth safer to say out loud. It's clarity around roles, decision rights, and handoffs so people don't have to guess or protect themselves. It's communication that reduces drag, feedback that develops without damaging, and connection that keeps the crew human when the work gets heavy.

This is also where your close-the-loop practices live, because trust doesn't die in hard news. Trust dies in unanswered feedback and vague leadership. Resilient and steady teams don't just "try harder." They reduce drag.

That's the whole point of this layer. You are not building resilience by asking people to endure more. You're building steadiness by designing how the team works when things are uncertain, stressful, or changing quickly. You're designing how the team stays aligned, and how they recover, and how they repair (Alliger et al., 2015).

Level 3: Environmental Steadiness (The Water)

This is Zone 5. It's the layer most leaders underestimate, because it's the one that forces you to face reality.

You can do everything "right" inside your team and still be operating in rough water. Culture shifts. Politics. Market pressure. Reorgs. Leadership changes. Burnout conditions. Toxic behaviors upstream.

You may not control those currents, but you can read them early and lead how your team responds.

At this level, steadiness is your ability to identify early warning signs before the team capsizes as I wrote about in Chapter 13. It's your ability to navigate the conflict I wrote about in Chapter 14 without letting it become identity. It's your ability to lead change without whiplash, as I address in this chapter. And yes, it includes managing up when you don't control the big calls, because sometimes the most stabilizing thing you can do for your team is secure clarity from the people who hold the decision rights.

You can't control every current, but you can lead how your team responds to it.

So, here's the definition of steady by design I want you to carry forward: it is when a leader builds a team that can absorb pressure without losing trust, clarity, health, or performance. It's when people can face hard change without panic, tell the truth without fear, recover without guilt, and keep moving without burning out.

Short-term resilience gets you through the week. Steady by design is what you build so your team can thrive through the year, and that is what we're doing in this book. We're moving from "How do I get through this?" to "How do I lead so my team doesn't get whiplash every time the water shifts?"

Because change is inevitable. Whiplash is not.

Steady by design is what you build so your team doesn't have to rely on adrenaline and survival strategies. But I also know this: when pressure hits, it rarely gives you a calendar invite. I know this from my 20 plus years of experience leading teams through reorgs, mergers and acquisitions, digital transformation, and yes, that layoff!

The moment you feel that surge, the moment you get the email, the moment you walk out of the meeting and realize things just changed, your team doesn't need you to have the perfect plan. They need you to be steady enough to keep the canoe from wobbling while you figure out the next right move.

That's why I'm pausing here to give you a practical playbook. This next section is not theory. It's what you do when the water turns fast and your nervous system wants to react. It's how you lead the first 72 hours, so your team doesn't spiral, your credibility doesn't wobble, and trust stays intact.

The Pressure Playbook

When a merger gets announced. When layoffs are rumored. When a reorg hits. When a new system drops and everything slows down. When leaders above you stop communicating. When your team is looking at you like, "Are we okay?"

In the first 72 hours, your job is not to become a therapist. Your job is to become a caring stabilizer.

Here are seven moves that reduce whiplash fast not because they make change disappear, but because they restore trust and direction. You may notice some from the previous chapters, and their cameo appearance here is meant to underline their importance when the pressure is high.

1. Name the water out loud

    Silence creates stories, and in uncertain waters, stories get dark quickly.

    Say something real. Not dramatic. Not performative. Just real.

    "I know this is a lot."

    "I know people are anxious."

    "I know the questions are coming faster than the answers."

    "I'm not going to pretend this is easy."

    When leaders don't name the emotional reality, teams feel alone in it. When you name it, you give the crew permission to stop hiding. You also endear them to you, because they see you are human and share in their emotions.

2. Use the three-part steadiness script

    During major change, people don't only need information. They need something steady to hold onto. You can't promise outcomes you don't control, but you can promise clarity, care, and follow-through.

Here is the script:

- "Here's what we know right now."
- "Here's what we don't know yet."
- "Here's what will stay true about how we lead and communicate while we figure it out."

That last line is where your values and North Star norms stop being just in your signature line and start being an anchor.

3. Tighten decision integrity, even if you can't share everything yet

One of the quickest ways to reduce whiplash is to reduce decision confusion.

If you can't share details, you still can share: what decision has been made versus what is still pending, who owns which decisions, when the next decision window is, and how you will communicate "decision alerts."

Your team can tolerate "we don't know yet" far better than they can tolerate leaders who sound unsure, inconsistent, or evasive.

4. Create one reliable communication rhythm (and protect it like it matters)

Your team doesn't need constant updates. They need predictable updates and fast clarity when something changes.

This is exactly why my LinkedIn poll result is so powerful. Nearly half of respondents chose: weekly updates + decision alerts (49%), and another 32% chose weekly consistent updates. Your people aren't begging for noise. They're begging for care and steadiness.

Here's what I've learned the hard way: if the people sponsoring the change are quiet, unclear, or hard to find, the change gets shaky fast. Prosci's research keeps pointing to the same reality, visible leadership sponsorship is one of the strongest drivers of successful change, and many organizations still say their sponsors aren't as ready or effective as they need to be (Horlick, 2025).

So don't overcomplicate it:

Pick a rhythm your team can count on.

Honor it and when something changes, communicate it quickly.

5. Protect capacity like it's part of the change plan (because it is)

In change, leaders often do the opposite of what teams need. They add more meetings. They increase urgency. They squeeze timelines. They assume people will "rise to the occasion."

But if you squeeze a team that's already running hot, you don't get excellence. You get erosion.

This is where your Recovery Rituals belong, inside the change conversation, not as a side note.

Say it plainly:

"We are not going to survive this season by grinding."

"We are going to survive by being smart about capacity."

"If something urgent comes in, something else pauses."

That one rule alone reduces whiplash because it restores a sense of control.

6. Close the loop fast, especially on what you can't do

The fastest way to lose trust in change is not bad news. It's unanswered questions. The less you leave unanswered, the more your team will feel steady and continue to move forward.

This is where the Close-the-Loop Tracker in Zone 4 becomes a change leadership tool, not just a listening tool.

Here's the line that makes it real:

"If we can't act on it, we'll still close the loop and tell you why."

This is dignity and care in action. Stop waiting to get the "perfect" answer or response. While you are waiting for perfect, your team is wondering whether or not you are the leader for the voyage.

7. Make the team's values and North Star norms visible again

Under pressure, teams forget who they are. They become reactive. They default into fear, blame, silence, perfectionism, gossip and not because they are "toxic," but because their environment is demanding protection moves.

So, bring the North Star back not as inspiration, but as operating guidance, a reminder of the shoreline. Here are examples of what you might say in the moment:

"Here's what stays true about how we treat each other."

"Here's what stays true about how we communicate."

"Here's what stays true about how we make decisions."

"Here's what stays true about how we repair when we miss."

Your norms become the stabilizers that prevent whiplash from becoming culture. Your North Star values reduce the wobble. Just because the wobble goes down does not mean people will not be anxious when the pressure is on. In those moments of anxiety, you might need some guidance on what NOT to say to your team. Let me help.

What Not to Say When People Are Anxious

This is where leaders accidentally light a match near gasoline. A few phrases that feel efficient to leaders can feel dismissive to teams:

"Don't worry about it."

"It'll all work out."

"Just focus on your job."

"This is above my pay grade."

"Nothing is changing" (when everyone knows something is changing).

You don't have to say the perfect thing. But you do have to say the honest thing.

Try these instead:

"I don't have the full answer yet, and I'm not going to speculate."

"What I can do is keep you updated and protect how we lead through it."

"If you're feeling distracted, that makes sense. Let's narrow the focus to what matters this week."

"I'm here. I'm not going anywhere. We'll walk through this in the open and together."

That's steadiness. That's leadership, and it is not easy. I have been transparent about how I did not always handle change and pressure around my team in the perfect way. I had to learn the hard way what my job really is: to be the steady, caring foundation my team can count on when the-you-know-what hits the fan! When I am that leader . . . when you are that leader, your team can become more agile and be willing and able to adapt to whatever comes your way with you as their protection against exhaustion.

Agility and Adaptability Without Exhaustion

There's a version of agility that's healthy. It's learning, adapting, and improving with the water. It's a team that can adjust course without losing its grip on the paddle, because they have one another.

Then, there's the exhausting version, and you already know what that feels like: constant pivots with no clarity, no closure, no "why," and no respect for capacity. It's when the canoe keeps turning, but no one can tell you where the shoreline is anymore. That's when people don't just get tired, they get cynical. They stop offering ideas. They start protecting themselves, and then the wobble becomes the operating system.

This isn't just a "soft" problem. It's a performance problem. Microsoft's Work Trend Index has reported that 80% of employees say they don't have enough time or energy to do their work

(Microsoft, 2025). When leaders ask for more adaptability on top of that reality, without changing anything else, what they're really asking for is depletion disguised as resilience.

Here is the part executive leaders expect from the leaders who report to them, whether they say it out loud or not: they want speed, yes, but they also want stability. They want you to keep execution moving *without* burning out your people or losing your best performers to quiet quitting or a job search. They want you to be the leader who can translate turbulence into traction.

That's why healthy agility has three non-negotiables, because you love structure, and because structure is how you keep the canoe steady when the water starts pushing back. Here are those non-negotiables:

- A clear shoreline, purpose and priorities
- Steady signals, communication and connection
- A visible system, decision rights, handoffs, and follow-through

When you have those, adaptability becomes possible without whiplash because now the team isn't guessing. They're steering.

The opposite is also true. When sponsors of change and senior leaders aren't clear and visible, change gets messy fast. Prosci's change research consistently points to sponsorship as the biggest contributor to change success, yet they also note that 50% of executives don't understand their sponsorship role and how to lead effective change (Prosci Singapore, 2025). Translation: teams get asked to "be agile" while leadership stays vague, inconsistent, or absent. That creates wobble, and wobble always costs more than leaders think it will. So, then we need to ask ourselves whether "be agile" is code for "do what we say when we say it and deal with all the consequences no matter what!" That is a sobering thing to think about.

In the canoe, the leader's job during change is not to make the water calm. It's to make the next stroke clear. It's to reduce drag by making decisions visible, priorities simple, and tradeoffs real, because nothing exhausts people faster than doing work that gets undone by the next pivot. I am getting exhausted just typing this!

When the current changes, most teams don't get clearer, they get louder. We start paddling harder. We add meetings. We send more messages. We "circle back" on the same issue three different ways and all of it can feel productive in the moment, but underneath it is usually the same thing: people are trying to find stability.

That's why I love the Ritz-Carlton example I shared a couple times in this book as a quiet, practical masterclass in healthy agility. Many people know them for service. What I want you to notice is the ritual behind the service: the short daily lineup. It's quick. It's consistent. And it keeps standards and priorities visible when the water is changing. Teams share what matters today and stories of what "great" looks like in action, not as a poster on the wall, but as real behaviors happening in real moments. That matters because it does two things at once: it tightens the standard so excellence stays clear, and it strengthens connection so people feel part of something shared.

In canoe language, the lineup is a steady rhythm. It's the beat that helps the crew stay in sync so change doesn't feel like chaos. When your team has a consistent ritual like that, you don't have to reinvent alignment every time the water shifts. People aren't left guessing what the priority is. They aren't filling silence with their own stories. They can adapt faster because the "what matters" is stable even when the conditions are not.

So, here's the question I want to leave you with: What is your version of a lineup? Not a meeting that drains people . . . a short, repeatable rhythm that makes the next right move obvious, because the goal is not constant motion. The goal is steady progress without whiplash.

And here's a simple *gut-check* you can use anytime you feel the "agility" conversation turning into whiplash:

If we take on this new urgent priority, what are we pausing, removing, or delaying so our people aren't carrying two full loads at once?

That's what real adaptability looks like, not endless pivots but tradeoffs, clarity, and a steadier canoe.

Here's the part that can feel frustrating: you can ask that tradeoff question, do the right things inside your team, and still watch people wobble. Not because your team is failing, but because the water around your team is still churning. Sometimes the whiplash isn't coming from poor execution. It's coming from decisions being made above you, messaging that keeps changing, or leaders who won't name what's true yet. That's when your job expands. You're not only leading down and across, you are leading up.

Managing Up to Calm the Waters (When You Don't Have Final Say)

If you don't have final authority over decisions that affect your team, you still have responsibility for their stability. That means you need a skill set many leaders avoid because it feels political: managing up.

I'm not talking about flattery. I'm not talking about "playing the game." I'm talking about advocating for clarity, capacity, and care so your team doesn't drown in ambiguity while leaders debate behind closed doors.

When senior leaders stay vague, the wobble shows up downstream. People start looking for boulders in the water. Rumors grow legs. High performers are forced to do it all, and your calendar fills up with emotional cleanup work you didn't budget for.

Managing up is how you make stability louder than pressure when you can't personally quiet the whole storm.

Managing up is:

- translating what's happening on the ground into decision-ready information
- asking for clarity in a way leaders can actually respond to

- naming the cost of delay without sounding dramatic
- protecting capacity by forcing tradeoffs
- creating a clean message your team can trust

Managing up is not:

- complaining
- pushing panic upward
- asking executives to "communicate more" without telling them what would help
- escalating emotion instead of reducing it

Here's the shift: don't go to senior leaders with "my team is anxious." Take my word on this one. Instead, go with something like, "Here are the three biggest wobble points, what they're costing us, and the decision we need."

When you put wobble into executive language, it stops being "feelings" and becomes what it is: a risk to execution, retention, and reputation. Now, you have their attention! Below are a couple real-world scenarios (code for things I have actually experienced and will never forget) that might help you bypass some of the headache and heartache I experienced not having this insight in advance.

Scenario 1: A merger/acquisition is announced, but regulatory constraints limit what can be shared.

Your team is spiraling because silence feels like danger.

What to say up:

"I know we can't share details yet, but we can share a steady cadence and a stable container. I'm asking for two things: a weekly update that confirms what's still true, and decision alerts within 24 hours when anything changes. Even a short message that says 'no new updates this week' reduces rumor."

What to ask for:

- a communication cadence you can promise (even if content is limited)
- a Q&A intake system + owner + response timeframe (so questions don't vanish)
- a "what we know / don't know / next checkpoint" statement you can reuse

Scenario 2: Reorg planning is happening, but leaders keep "working the plan" behind the scenes while teams wait.

Your team is spending energy guessing and updating resumes instead of doing work. Typing this scenario truly makes me want to scream! Please choose to be the more socially aware leader and understand the impact of the closed-door meetings.

What to say up:

"The longer this sits in limbo, the more we pay for it in distraction and exits. I'm not asking for a perfect org chart today. I'm asking for what we can stabilize right now: decision timelines, what won't change, and how we'll handle role uncertainty in the interim."

What to ask for:

- a clear timeline with checkpoints (even if the final answer isn't ready)
- temporary role clarity ("for the next 30 days, decision rights sit here")
- permission to pause or reprioritize work that will likely be undone

The following table summarizes the content of this Managing Up section. You can use it to help you decide the appropriate thing to say and what specific scenario to say it in.

Managing Up During Change: Scenarios, Language, and What to Ask For

Scenario in the water	What your team is experiencing	What to say to senior leaders (in your voice)	What to ask for (so you can calm the waters)
Regulatory silence (acquisition, legal hold)	Rumors, fear, constant "any updates?"	"We can't share everything, but we can share steadiness. Silence creates stories. Let's set a cadence and a container."	Weekly update + decision alerts, Q&A intake with owner + response expectation, next checkpoint date
Reorg ambiguity	People guessing roles, productivity drag	"Clarity isn't optional right now. Even temporary clarity reduces wobble."	Timeline with checkpoints, interim decision rights, what stays stable for 30–60 days
Layoff anxiety (no confirmation yet)	Hypervigilance, disengagement	"We can't promise outcomes, but we can promise dignity and follow-through. The vacuum is costing us."	Messaging boundaries (what can/can't be said), manager talking points, support resources, cadence
Too many priorities	People overloaded, pack mule effect	"We are asking for agility without making tradeoffs. That becomes exhaustion."	Stop/Start list, tradeoff rule, top 3 priorities, what gets paused
Leaders saying different things	Confusion, cynicism, "they're hiding"	"We need one message and one source of truth. Mixed signals create drag."	Single narrative, comms owner, updated FAQ, escalation path for questions
Culture feels toxic at the top	Fear, CYA behavior, low trust	"The behavior upstream becomes the weather downstream. My team is adapting by protecting themselves."	Clear expectations for leader behavior, enforcement plan, safe reporting channel, visible accountability
Managers are the shock absorbers	Middle leaders burning out	"We are carrying the emotional load of uncertainty. If we don't protect manager capacity, the system breaks."	Manager support rhythm, talking points, decision turnaround time, fewer cascading meetings
A big change is coming "soon"	Endless waiting, fatigue	"Waiting is a stressor. If we can't decide today, we need a date when we will."	Decision date, interim operating rules, what will not change until then

If you want one repeatable formula, use this. It's calm, direct, and executive-friendly:

1. "Here's what I'm seeing on the ground."
2. "Here's the wobble it's creating (drag, risk, distraction, exits)."
3. "Here's what I need from you to stabilize it."
4. "Here's what I'll own once you decide."

Example:

"Here's what I'm seeing: the team is spending more time guessing than executing. The wobble is rework and rising attrition risk. What I need is a weekly update cadence and a timeline checkpoint we can count on. Once we have that, I'll own the team communication, the Q&A loop, and the operating rhythm."

I'm flashing back again to that same season I've mentioned before, the merged environment, the one that eventually ended with me being laid off alongside hundreds of other people.

But before that happened, I made a decision that didn't feel natural for me at the time. I decided to carry something on my shoulders that technically wasn't in my job description. I became, in my own way, a culture bearer. A culture ambassador. Not because I thought I could "fix everything," but because I could see the culture suffering in real time, and I couldn't unsee it.

Communication was thin. Trust was even thinner. Nobody trusted anybody, and the silence in the building wasn't calm silence. It was fear silence. People weren't talking, but they were absolutely assuming. You could feel it in the hallways. You could feel it in meetings. You could feel it in how people avoided eye contact and kept their heads down. Everyone was scanning for signs they might lose their job, and because nobody was naming anything out loud, the tension just thickened and spread.

So, I co-created an Employee Engagement Council.

It started with a handful of people from different parts of the merged organization, some in our office and some not, who had come to me saying some version of, "This is hard. I want to help. What can we do to make this work?" They didn't want to sit in the uncertainty and just complain about it. They wanted to be part of stabilizing it.

So, I brought them together.

That council became our way of saying, "we're not going to wait for permission to care. We're not going to wait for someone at the top to finally communicate perfectly before we act like leaders where we stand. We're going to be the change we keep hoping someone else will deliver."

We held listening sessions. We hosted roundtables. We collected what people were worried about, what they needed, what was breaking trust, what was making the work harder than it had to be. And then I took those themes and brought them to the leaders who were steering the merger.

Did that mean everything suddenly became perfect? No. Let me be very clear about that.

There were still plenty of things happening behind closed doors that I didn't know about. The communication still wasn't ideal. The uncertainty didn't magically disappear. There were no roses blooming in the hallway and no dramatic "and then everyone trusted each other" ending.

But here's what did happen: I felt more self-empowered, and I watched other people feel it too.

At a time when the environment was designed, unintentionally or not, to make people feel helpless, we created a pocket of agency. We created a way for people to use their voices without needing permission for every single step. We created movement in a season that felt frozen.

And that matters.

Because when the water is rough, the leader doesn't always get final say. Sometimes you can't make the big decisions. Sometimes you can't reveal what you know. Sometimes you're not the one holding the legal, regulatory, or executive authority.

But you can still steady the canoe.

You can still name what's true to someone who can act.

You can still create structure that gives people voice and dignity.

You can still build a rhythm that reduces fear and increases agency.

You can still protect your team from taking on water emotionally, even when the broader environment is messy.

And even though that chapter of my career ended the way it ended, I can say this: I did my part. I refused to let the culture collapse on my watch without trying to stabilize it, and in the middle of a season that could have made me feel powerless, choosing action made me feel steady again.

That's the point I want you to take with you: when you don't have full control of the water, you can still control how you show up in it, and that, all by itself, reduces wobble.

Paddle: Pressure-Proof the Team

A 7-minute weekly reset that reduces wobble.

1. **Name the water (1 minute)**

   Leader: "What's changing or pressurizing us this week?"

2. **Wobble scan (3 minutes)**

   Go around fast. Each person answers:

   - "One thing creating drag is. . ."
   - "One thing making the team feel shaky is. . ."

3. **Make 3 stabilizing decisions (2 minutes)**

   As a leader, lock these in out loud:

   - **Priority:** "This week, our top 1 focus is ___."
   - **Tradeoff:** "To protect capacity, we are pausing ___."
   - **Owner:** "The decision/next step on ___ is owned by ___ by (date)."

4. **Close the loop promise (1 minute)**

   Leader: "Here's what I heard. Here's what we're doing. Here's when you'll get an update."

Back to the Canoe

When the team is tired of "one more change," don't just tell them to be resilient. Remind them of the shoreline. Remind them of the rhythm. Remind them that they were built to handle hard water, and that your job is to make sure they don't have to do it alone.

And now we're ready for the conclusion, because this is the last leadership truth I want to leave you with: you don't create an unshakable team by removing uncertainty. You create an unshakable team by leading with steadiness when uncertainty shows up.

Conclusion: Steady Enough to Lead

Let me start with a confession that might surprise you, given how much I've used the canoe as a metaphor in this book.

I would not have even gotten into the canoe.

I don't love being on the water. Not like that. It's not that I can't appreciate a lake or a beautiful day outdoors. It's that being on the water pokes at my relationship with control. The moment you're out there, you feel it. You are no longer fully in charge of the conditions. The current shifts. The wind changes. The water does what it does. My stomach gets nervous, because my body knows I can't predict everything, and it reacts, which is probably why this story has never left me.

My son was fearless and courageous enough to get into the canoe in the first place. He didn't stand on the shore calculating what could go wrong. He climbed in. Then, when the wobble started, he did what most humans do when we're in something we can't fully control. He felt it in his body first. His system registered uncertainty, and his mind started scanning for what it meant. Then, he made it back to shore with the help of my husband.

I was the first person he spoke to when he got off and got back on dry land. That moment still rings true for me, because what he described to me then is what I hear from leaders all the time now: the mix of adrenaline and doubt, the desire to do well, the tension of not knowing what the water will do next, and the quiet realization that the only way forward is not through control, but through trusting the team.

I want you to hold that thought as we close, because the irony of the story is this.

Eight years later, that same boy is now a midshipman at the United States Naval Academy.

What still makes me smile when I say that out loud is that he didn't just get into one academy. He had options. He got into three academies! He could have chosen a path that kept him away from the water if he wanted to. Yet, he chose the one that puts him on the water.

I don't know about you, but I can't help but see meaning in that.

Maybe, he realized the water wasn't so bad. Maybe, he realized that wobble is not danger; it's information. Maybe, he realized that the ability to steady yourself and stay in rhythm with a crew matters more than being able to control the conditions. Maybe, he learned, early, that excellence isn't an individual sport. It's a team practice. And maybe, even at 10 years old, something in him understood what so many leaders must learn the hard way: relying on a team is not weakness. It's the only way to do hard things well for a long time.

That's why I've used the canoe in this book. Not because I'm trying to make you love the water. I'm not sure I do either. I've used it because leadership now feels like water. The pace of change isn't slowing down. Technology isn't waiting for anyone to catch up. Work isn't getting simpler. Many organizations are asking people to do more with less while also acting surprised when burnout shows up and engagement is low. People aren't leaving their humanity at the door when they walk into work. They're bringing their nervous systems, their stress responses, their uncertainty, their hopes, their fatigue, their pride, and their need to matter into meetings, deadlines, and decisions.

The water is the reality you are leading in.

And here is the truth I want to say plainly as we close: the goal is not to eliminate wobble. The goal is to build the kind of team that can feel wobble without tipping. The goal is to build a crew and a system and a rhythm strong enough that even when the water is rough, you stay upright.

Unshakable is not unbreakable.

Unshakable is being steady enough, and caring enough, to keep the team from capsizing when the pressure never stops.

If you take nothing else from this book, I want you to take that distinction with you. A lot of leaders hear "unshakable" and think it means you never struggle, you never doubt, you never feel the stress in your body, you never wobble. That's not what I mean. What I mean is that wobble does not have to take you down. Wobble is part of the human experience of change, complexity, and pressure. Wobble happens when the stakes feel high and the conditions feel uncertain.

The difference is what you do next.

That's why I've called it wobble throughout this book. Wobble is feedback. It's an early warning sign. It's your first signal that something needs attention before it becomes expensive. Wobble shows up in tone, in silence, in frustration, in cynicism, in perfectionism, in disengagement, in gossip, in conflict, in exhaustion, and sometimes in exit.

Wobble doesn't always look dramatic. Sometimes it looks like a team that is still producing but no longer believes. Sometimes it looks like a team that is still delivering but quietly depleted. Sometimes it looks like people saying "yes" while their bodies and hearts are saying "no."

The strongest leaders don't shame wobble. They don't ignore it. They don't punish it.

They read it.

They name it.

They respond to it.

They do that by strengthening the five zones. Not because zones are cute categories. Because teams don't capsize for one reason. They capsize because multiple layers weaken at once. When purpose gets fuzzy, people drift. When trust thins, people protect themselves. When systems are unclear, drag multiplies. When rhythm disappears, burnout rises. When conditions get rough and no one names what's happening, fear starts steering the canoe.

That's why this book is not another resilience book.

This book is steady by design.

It's the difference between hoping your team holds together and building a team that is designed to hold steady. It's the difference between asking people to "bounce back" and building the kind of structure, trust, rhythm, and clarity that makes recovery normal. It's the difference between a team that survives because they're tough and a team that sustains excellence because the system supports the humans doing the work.

Zone 1 is The Shoreline. It is purpose and priorities. When the water gets rough, the shoreline is what keeps you from paddling hard in the wrong direction. It's what gives people a point of reference when everything is changing. When leaders get shaky, they often talk more but say less. They fill space with activity, meetings, and updates that don't restore clarity. Zone 1 is where you return to what matters most and make it visible again, so the team can move with focus instead of panic.

Zone 2 is The Crew. It is trust and care. Trust is reliability, and care is dignity. Psychological safety is the environment that makes truth possible early enough to prevent damage. If Zone 2 is strong, people tell the truth sooner, risks surface earlier, and recovery happens faster. If Zone 2 is weak, people start protecting themselves, hiding problems, and speaking sideways because the direct path doesn't feel safe. Zone 2 is where you build a team that can speak honestly without fear and stay connected even when pressure rises.

Zone 3 is The Canoe. It is systems and structure. Decision rights, ownership, handoffs, follow-through, operating rhythm—these are not cold mechanics. They are stabilizers. Systems are caring because they reduce guessing. They reduce rework. They reduce the invisible friction that drains energy and creates burnout. When Zone 3 is strong, you protect excellence not by pushing harder, but by reducing drag.

Zone 4 is The Signal. It is communication and connection. Zone 4 is where you replace rumor with steadiness, fear with clarity, and disconnection with human leadership. It's where listening becomes an operating system, closing the loop becomes trust infrastructure, feedback becomes development, and connection becomes a performance strategy. The Signal is what keeps the canoe moving without burning out the crew.

Zone 5 is The Water. It is culture and conditions. This is where you stop pretending the environment doesn't matter. You read the water early. You name the macro pressures. You address toxicity. You navigate conflict without capsizing. You lead change without whiplash. You manage up when you don't have final say. You protect your team from currents they did not create. You cannot control every condition, but you can absolutely lead how your team responds to conditions.

And here's the most important truth beneath all five zones.

Your relationship with your team is completely interconnected.

You don't just lead people; you shape the conditions they work in. They don't just "follow your direction"; they reflect your steadiness back to you. When the team can rely on you to be a stabilizing force, you can then rely on them to do hard things from a place of excellence. When the team trusts you, they take risks earlier, tell the truth sooner, and stay engaged longer. When they feel cared for, they recover faster and bring more of their best selves to the work. When they have clarity, they stop thrashing and start moving in sync.

You succeed together. You sustain together.

That's why my son's story matters here at the end. His decision to choose the Naval Academy over the other academies tells me something that leaders need to hear right now: the water doesn't scare the people who learn how to trust their crew, trust their training, and trust their ability to respond to wobble without panic. The water doesn't scare the people who know they don't have to control everything to lead well. The water doesn't scare the people who understand that excellence is sustained through the team, not through the leader's individual heroics.

If you're reading this and thinking, "I'm not sure I'm that leader," I want to offer you something honest and freeing.

You don't have to suddenly become fearless. You don't have to love the water. You don't have to feel perfectly confident. You just have to become more intentional. You have to decide that wobble is information, not indictment. You have to decide that care isn't optional, and clarity isn't optional, and follow-through isn't optional. You have to decide that your team's humanity is not an inconvenience to performance. It is the container where excellence either lives or dies.

This is also where I want to name something you might have noticed: I chose to focus more on "steady" than "strong." People sometimes wonder why. Here's why. "Strong" can sound unfazed. It can sound like you're supposed to be untouchable, unbothered, unwobble-able. That isn't the kind of leadership most teams need right now. Teams don't need a leader who never feels anything. They need a leader who can feel what's real and still stay grounded. Steadiness has humanness inside of it. Steadiness is calm, centeredness, and being a stabilizing force, especially in a world where so many nervous systems are already running off the rails because of rapid change and everything happening in the macro environment. I'm not saying strong is overrated. I'm saying steadiness is underrated, and I believe that a steady, caring leader is exactly what this moment and the foreseeable future requires.

That's why I don't want you to treat this book like a one-time read.

I want you to treat it like a navigation guide.

Mark it up with highlighters and sticky notes. Dog-ear the pages. Write in the margins. Bring it into a leadership team meeting. Share a tool with your peers. Pass a copy to another leader you care about. If you're leading a team right now, consider buying a copy for one or two of your leaders and using it as a shared language. Because the truth is, many of the lessons in this book were hard-earned or hard-learned, by me and by others. I wrote them down so you don't have to keep learning the hard way.

When leaders everywhere do this, when they stop treating trust as optional, and connection as extra, and listening as soft, and recovery as weakness, something bigger happens. You become part of a shift in leadership. A shift away from grind culture as a badge of honor. A shift away from silence being mistaken as alignment. A shift away from "just deal with it" leadership. A shift toward teams that can tell the truth early, recover on purpose, and sustain excellence without losing themselves.

Yes, you leave a legacy, not only the kind that shows up on your resume, but the kind that also shows up in people. In the people who learned how to lead because you showed them. In the people who stayed because you steadied the canoe. In the people who found their voice because you closed the loop. In the people who grew because feedback felt developmental, not judgmental. In the people who kept going because you made stability louder than fear.

So Where Do You Go from Here?

Start with the Unshakable Team Stability Scan from the beginning of the book if you haven't already. Let it show you where your team is strong and where it's wobbling. Choose two or three moves, just two or three, that you can own in the next 30 days. Make them visible. Tell your team what you're working on. Invite them into the rhythm. Ask for feedback. Close the loop. Repeat.

Then, take the **Steadiness Index** assessment by scanning the QR code a few pages following this conclusion to get a baseline of your leadership steadiness and come back to it periodically to see how you are improving. That's how culture shifts. That's how trust strengthens. That's how steadiness becomes normal.

Because unshakable isn't a title you earn once.

Unshakable is a practice you return to again and again.

When the team is tired of one more change, when the pressure is in the water, when the environment feels shaky and the canoe starts to wobble, you will know what to do. You'll steady yourself first. You'll return to the shoreline. You'll care for the crew. You'll rely on the canoe you've built. You'll remain consistent with the signals. You'll read the water, and you'll keep moving forward together.

That is the work. That is leadership. That is how excellence becomes sustainable.

If you ever feel the canoe wobble and wonder whether you're built for these waters, remember this: I'm right here with you, cheering you on as you steady, lead, and build the Unshakable Team your people deserve.

Take the Steadiness Index™ Assessment

Scan the QR code below to discover where you are strongest, where pressure may be creating instability, and which dimension to strengthen next.

https://heatheryounger.com/thesteadinessindex/

The Measure of Leadership Stability Under Pressure

Resilience has taught us to bounce back.

But today's leaders and teams need more than the ability to recover after pressure.

They need the ability to stay grounded, connected, aligned, and adaptive while the pressure is still unfolding.

That is steadiness.

The **Steadiness Index** measures the leadership capacity behind an unshakable team: the ability to create stability without becoming rigid, offer care without avoiding accountability, and help people move forward with clarity when conditions are uncertain.

Steadiness is not about being calm every second.

It is not about pretending pressure does not exist.

It is about how leaders and teams think, communicate, decide, recover, and stay connected when the stakes are high.

The Steadiness Index is built around five dimensions:

1. **Regulated Presence**

   The ability to steady yourself before you steady the room.

2. **Clear Discernment**

   The ability to separate facts from fear and return to what matters most.

3. **Trustworthy Connection**

   The ability to create trust through listening, care, honesty, consistency, and accountability.

4. **Adaptive Alignment**

   The ability to help people adjust, decide, and move forward together when conditions change.

5. **Sustainable Renewal**

   The ability to restore capacity, repair trust, and learn from pressure before depletion becomes the culture.

Together, these five dimensions connect the full arc of Unshakable Leadership™.

The goal is not to become a leader who is never shaken.

The goal is to become the kind of leader others can count on when everything around them is shifting.

That is what helps a team become unshakable.

Employee Fanatix 2025 Team Culture Survey

Complete Report with Appendix A (Book Citation Pack)—Embedded Visual Graphs

Study year: 2025 | Combined dataset n = 535 | Prepared by Employee Fanatix

Key Cited Finding

In our firm's Employee Fanatix 2025 Team Culture Survey (EF25, n = 535), ambiguous roles ranked among the top contributors to burnout (25.4% selected this). On the solution side, over half of respondents (55.3%) pointed to alignment and clarity—defined as clear roles/expectations or clearer communication—as critical fixes (see Charts 2 and 3; Employee Fanatix, 2025; Appendix A, Table 1).

Visual Findings

Chart 1—Emotional Exhaustion by Work Setup

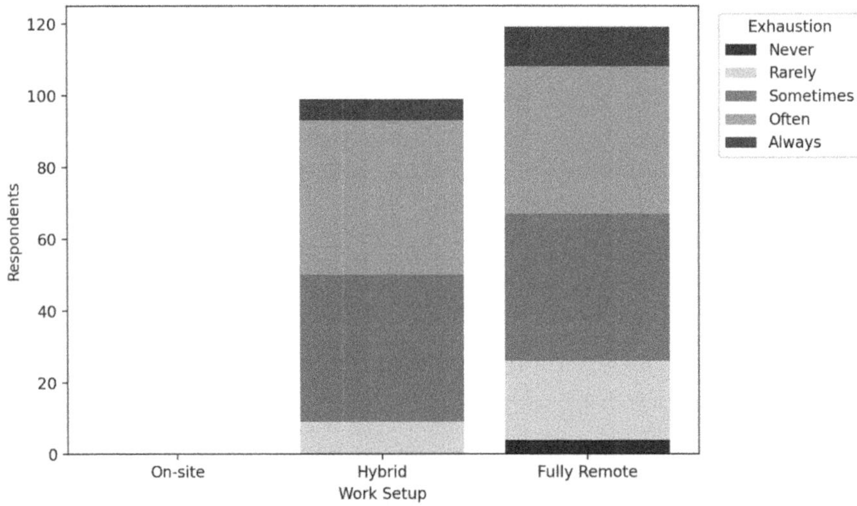

Distribution of emotional exhaustion across on-site, hybrid, and fully remote roles. Source: Employee Fanatix, EF25 (2025).

Chart 2—Top Burnout Contributors

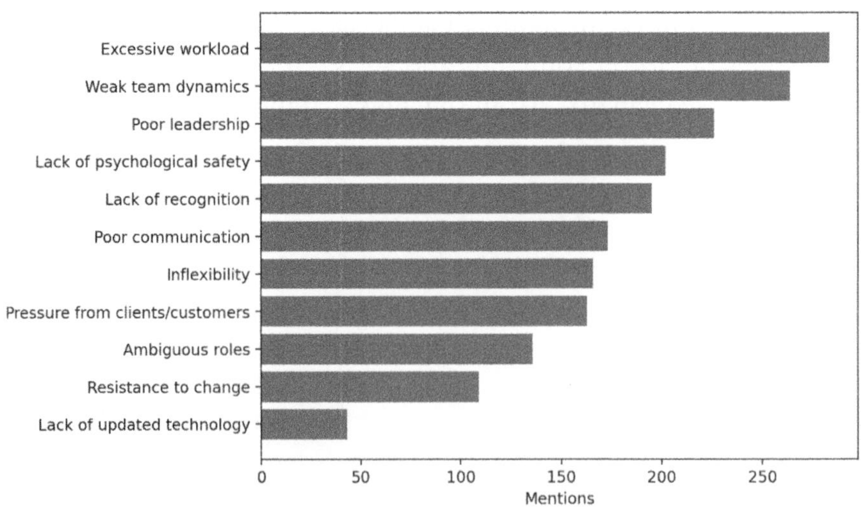

Most frequently cited burnout drivers, including ambiguous roles. Source: Employee Fanatix, EF25 (2025).

Chart 3—Employee-Requested Changes to Reduce Burnout

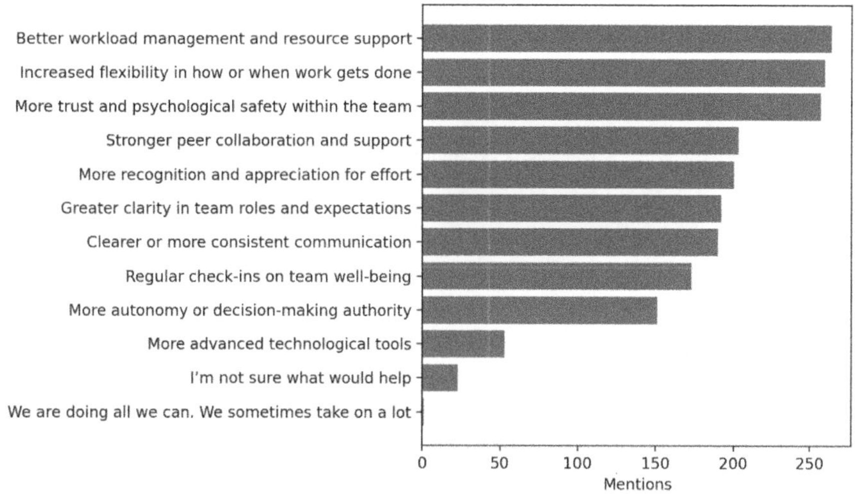

Most requested changes, including clarity in roles/expectations and clearer communication. Source: Employee Fanatix, EF25 (2025).

Chart 4—Average Exhaustion Versus Belief AI Can Help

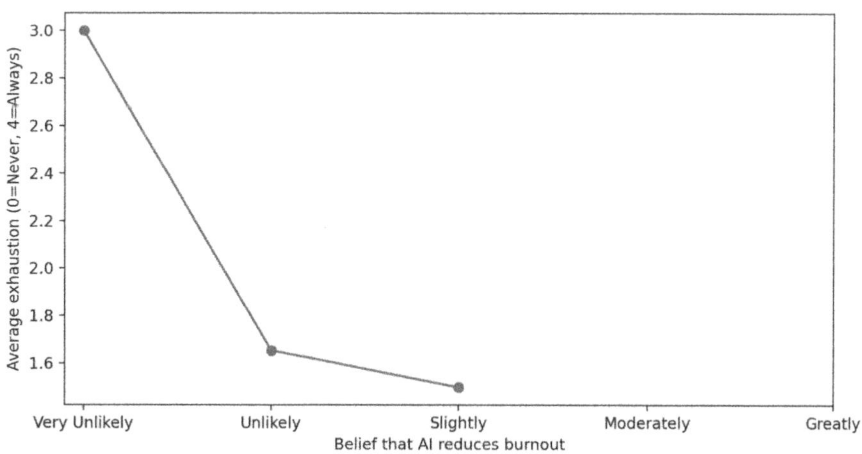

Average exhaustion decreases as belief that AI can help increases. Source: Employee Fanatix, EF25 (2025).

Appendix A—Book Citation Pack

Chart 2—Top Burnout Contributors

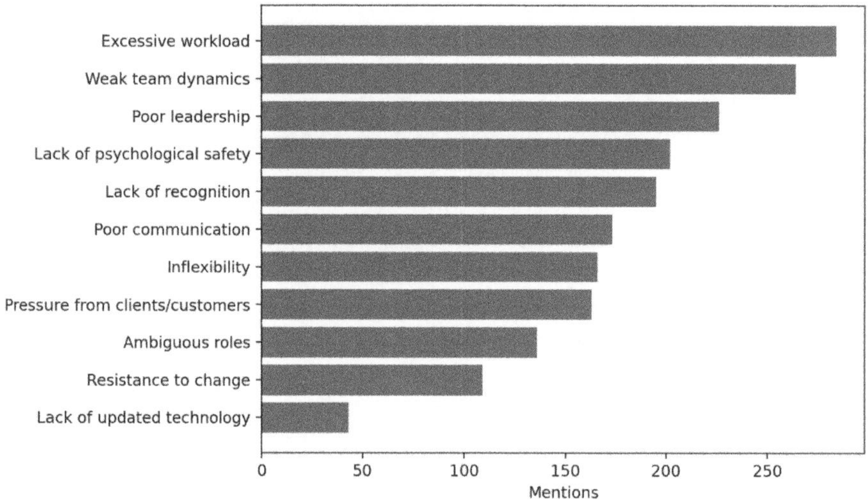

Most frequently cited burnout drivers, including ambiguous roles. Source: Employee Fanatix, EF25 (2025).

Chart 3—Employee-Requested Changes to Reduce Burnout

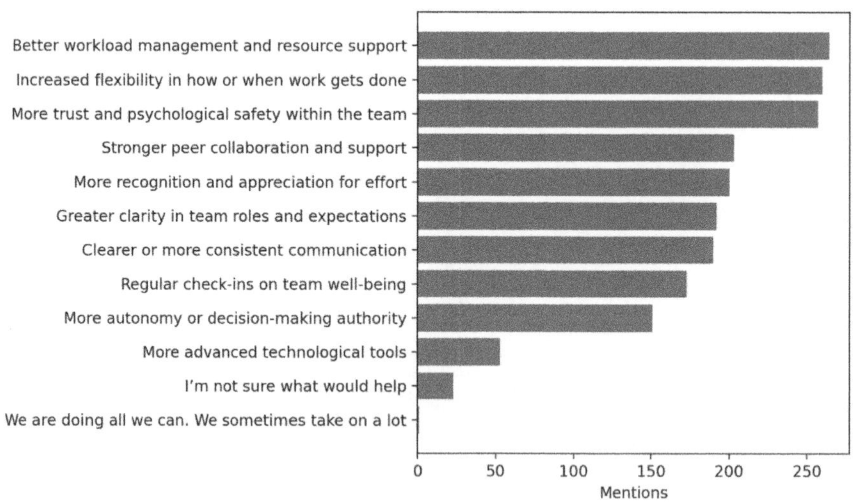

Most requested changes, including clarity in roles/expectations and clearer communication. Source: Employee Fanatix, EF25 (2025).

Chart 1—Emotional Exhaustion by Work Setup

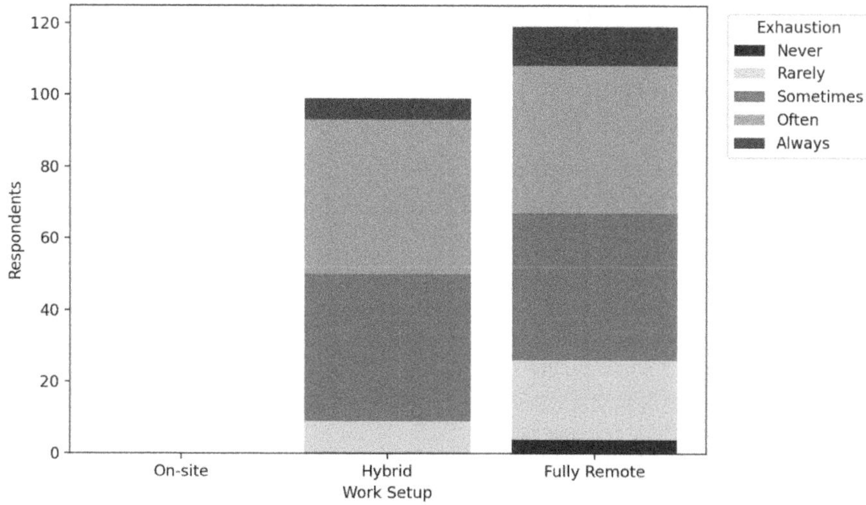

Distribution of emotional exhaustion across on-site, hybrid, and fully remote roles. Source: Employee Fanatix, EF25 (2025).

Chart 4—Average Exhaustion Versus Belief AI Can Help

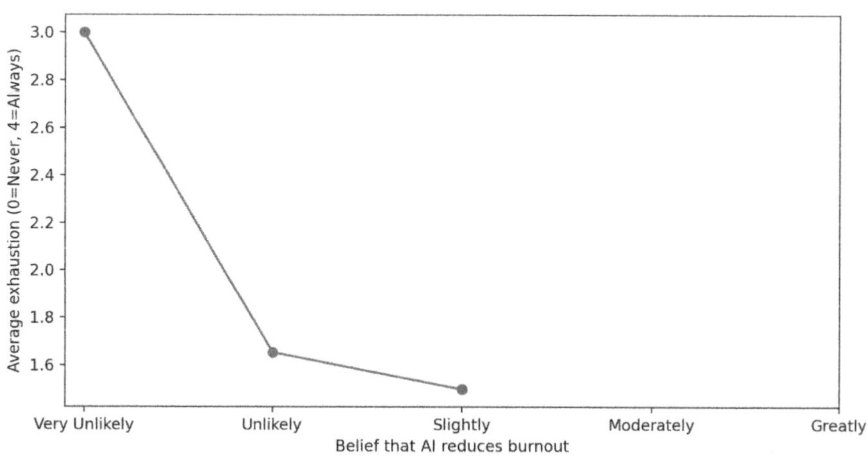

Average exhaustion decreases as belief that AI can help increases. Source: Employee Fanatix, EF25 (2025).

Table 1—Calculation Notes for Alignment and Clarity

Operational definition used for "alignment and clarity": respondents who selected either "Greater clarity in team roles and expectations" OR "Clearer or more consistent communication" on the multi-select fixes question. Unique respondents are counted once.

Item	Respondents (n)	Percent of sample (%)
Ambiguous roles (burnout contributor)	136	25.4
Greater clarity in team roles and expectations	192	35.9
Clearer or more consistent communication	190	35.5
Either clarity or communication (unique respondents)	296	55.3

Recommended Citation

Employee Fanatix 2025 Team Culture Survey. Appendix A, Charts 2–3 and Table 1.

References

Alliger, G. M., Cerasoli, C. P., Tannenbaum, S. I., and Vessey, W. B. (2015). "Team resilience: how teams flourish under pressure." *Organizational Dynamics*, 44(3), 176–184, https://doi.org/10.1016/j.orgdyn.2015.05.003

American Psychological Association. (2023). 2023 Work in America™ Survey. https://www.apa.org/pubs/reports/work-in-america/2023-workplace-health-well-being.

An Introduction to the National Incident Management System. (2020). FEMA. https://training.fema.gov/emiweb/is/is700b/student%20manual/smis0700b.pdf.

Atlassian. (n.d.a.). Audit Team Meetings. *Team Playbook*. https://www.atlassian.com/team-playbook/plays/audit-your-meetings

Atlassian. (n.d.b.). Team Communication Norms. *Team Playbook*. https://www.atlassian.com/team-playbook/plays/team-communication-norms

Barsade, S. G., Coutifaris, C. G. V., and Pillemer, J. (2018). "Emotional contagion in organizational life." *Research in Organizational Behavior*, 38, 137–151, ISSN 0191-3085, https://doi.org/10.1016/j.riob.2018.11.005.

BetterUp. (2019). BetterUp's New, Industry-Leading Research Shows Companies That Fail at Belonging Lose Tens of Millions in Revenue. *BetterUp*. https://www.betterup.com/press/betterups-new-industry-leading-research-shows-companies-that-fail-at-belonging-lose-tens-of-millions-in-revenue

Catmull, E. (2014). Inside The Pixar Braintrust. *Fast Company*. https://www.fastcompany.com/3027135/inside-the-pixar-braintrust.

Center for the Developing Child. (n.d.). Toxic Stress. https://developingchild.harvard.edu/key-concept/toxic-stress/

Codd, E. (2024). Mental Health at Work: Eight Reasons Employers Can't Ignore It. *Deloitte*. https://www.deloitte.com/hu/en/about/people/blogs/mental-health-at-work.html

Covey, S. (2008). *The Speed of Trust: The One Thing That Changes Everything*. The Free Press.

Dehoff, K. and Loehr, J. (2007). Innovation and Agility. *Tech & Innovation*. https://www.strategy-business.com/article/07208

Doerr, J. (2025). Why Adobe Killed Performance Reviews. *What Matters*. https://www.whatmatters.com/articles/why-adobe-killed-performance-reviews

Edmondson, A. (2018). *The Fearless Organization: Creating Psychological Safety in the Workplace for Learning, Innovation, and Growth*. Wiley.

Efron, L. (2022). "Are Your Company Values More Than Just Words?" *Gallup Workplace*. https://www.gallup.com/workplace/406418/company-values-words.aspx

Eisenberger, N. I., Liberman, M. D., and Williams, K. D. (2003). "Does rejection hurt? An FMRI study of social exclusion." *Science*. https://doi.org/10.1126/science.1091062

Farquhar, S. (2021). "Our Founders Announce a Giant Leap in Remote Work." *Product and News*. https://www.atlassian.com/blog/our-founders-announce-a-giant-leap-in-remote-work

FEMA. (2012). Incident Action Planning Guide. *FEMA*. https://www.dco.uscg.mil/Portals/9/CG-5R/nsarc/FEMA%20Incident%20Action%20Planning%20Guide%20%28IAP%29.pdf.

Grupe, D. W. and Nitschke, J. B. (2013). "Uncertainty and anticipation in anxiety: an integrated neurobiological and psychological perspective." *Nature Reviews. Neuroscience*, 14(7), 488–501. https://doi.org/10.1038/nrn3524

Harter, J. (2025). U.S. Employee Engagement Declines From 2020 Peak. *Gallup*. https://www.gallup.com/workplace/701486/employee-engagement-declines-2020-peak.aspx

Harter, J. (2026). Span of Control: What's the Optimal Team Size for Managers? *Gallup*. https://www.gallup.com/workplace/700718/span-control-optimal-team-size-managers.aspx

Horlick, A. (2025). Your Change Management Checklist: 8 Critical Elements for Transformation Success. *Prosci*. https://www.prosci.com/blog/checklist-for-your-change-management-approach

Jenkins, L. (2012). "With No Time to Waste, Lakers Make Right Decision in Firing Mike Brown." https://www.si.com/more-sports/2012/11/10/lakers-brown-firing-necessary-warriors.

Kim, H. and Kim, E. G. (2021). "A meta-analysis on predictors of turnover intention of hospital nurses in South Korea (2000-2020)." *NursingOpen*. https://doi.org/10.1002/nop2.872.

Lorenz, E. (2022). How to Bridge the Generational Gap in Recognition. *Gallup Workplace*. https://www.gallup.com/workplace/396470/bridge-generational-gap-recognition.aspx

Mayer, K. (2024). Incivility's Cost to Employers: $2 Billion a Day. *SHRM*. https://www.shrm.org/topics-tools/news/employee-relations/incivility-s-cost-to-employers---2-billion-a-day

McEwen, B. S. (2017). Neurobiological and systematic effects of chronic stress. *SageJournals*. https://journals.sagepub.com/doi/10.1177/2470547017692328

McKinsey Transformations. (2019). Mind-sets matter in transformations: A conversation with Jon Garcia. *McKinsey*. https://www.mckinsey.com/capabilities/transformation/our-insights/mind-sets-matter-in-transformations-a-conversation-with-jon-garcia

Microsoft. (2025). Microsoft's 2025 Work Trend Index Report Reveals the Rise of the Frontier Firm, Marking a New Era of Workforce Dynamics.

https://news.microsoft.com/en-cee/2025/04/24/microsofts-2025-work-trend-index-report-reveals-the-rise-of-the-frontier-firm-marking-a-new-era-of-workforce-dynamics-3

Microsoft. (2026). Work Trend Index Annual Report 2025: The year the Frontier Firm is born. https://www.microsoft.com/en-us/worklab/work-trend-index/2025-the-year-the-frontier-firm-is-born

NASA History Office. (2011). "Detailed Chronology of Events Surrounding the Apollo 13 Accident." *NASA*. https://www.nasa.gov/history/detailed-chronology-of-events-surrounding-the-apollo-13-accident

Piccotti, T. (2025). The Apollo 13 Rescue Captivated the World. It Took Years for the True Tale to Be Told Onscreen. Biography. https://www.biography.com/history-culture/a65639778/onscreen-history-behind-apollo-13.

Porath, C. and Pearson, C. (2013). The Price of Incivility. *Harvard Business Review*. https://www.qualitymanagementinstitute.com/images/hrsolutions/HBR-ThePriceofIncivility.pdf

Prosci Singapore. (2025). 3 Tips to Successfully Engage Reluctant Sponsors of Change. *Prosci*. https://www.prosci.com/blog/3-tips-to-successfully-engage-reluctant-sponsors-of-change

Ries, E. (2011). How DropBox Started as a Minimal Viable Product. *TechCrunch*. https://techcrunch.com/2011/10/19/dropbox-minimal-viable-product/.

Robison, J. (2020). Answer 'Yes' to Your Employees' Biggest Question. *Gallup Clifton Strengths*. https://www.gallup.com/cliftonstrengths/en/320273/answer-yes-employees-biggest-question.aspx

Rosen, et al. (n.d.). Meet the #1 barrier to productivity. *Atlassian*. https://www.atlassian.com/blog/workplace-woes-meetings

Stechschulte, N. (2024). Building Change Management Resilience for Your and Your Team. *Gartner Human Resources*. https://www.gartner.com/en/articles/building-change-management-resilience-for-you-and-your-team

Stephens, J. P., Heaphy, E., and Dutton, J. E. (2012). "High-quality connections." In K. S. Cameron & G. M. Spreitzer (Eds.), *The Oxford Handbook of Positive Organizational Scholarship* (pp. 385–399). Oxford University Press.

Urai, A. E., Braun, A., and Donner, T. H. (2017). "Pupil-linked arousal is driven by decision uncertainty and alters serial choice bias." *Nature Communications*, *8*(1). https://doi.org/10.1038/ncomms14637

Warren, C. (2014). Suite Success. *Insigniam Quarterly*. https://insigniam.com/wp-content/uploads/2014/12/suite.pdf

World Health Organization. (2019). Burn-Out an 'Occupational Phenomenon': International Classification of Diseases. https://www.who.int/news/item/28-05-2019-burn-out-an-occupational-phenomenon-international-classification-of-diseases.

Younger, H. R. (2021). *The Art of Caring Leadership: How Leading with Heart Uplifts Teams and Organizations*. Berrett-Koehler Publishers.

Younger, H. R. (2026). Turning Setbacks into Strength. The 3 Types of Failure and How to Bounce Back. *Becoming Unshakable with Heather R. Younger*. https://podcasts.apple.com/us/podcast/turning-setbacks-into-strength-the-3-types-of/id1366572251?i=1000750082153

Acknowledgments

To the Wiley team: Amanda Pyne, thank you for your support. I truly appreciate your candid advice and the way you respond to my ideas. It means a lot. Shannon Vargo, thank you for your openness to meet me where I was and let me change the title and subtitle of this book mid-stream. I think it was the best decision we could make. Tom Dinse, thank you for helping me develop my ideas and bring this book to life. This is our second book together, and I cannot think of a better partner. Ryan Flahive and Trinity Crompton for making sure this book is positioned for what the market needs. Sangeetha Suresh, thank you for your contributions and for helping make this book the best it can be and for working with me on our second book. And to everyone else at Wiley who worked behind the scenes on this project, including editorial, production, marketing, design, and the cover team, thank you. I am grateful for your care, your craftsmanship, and the many details you handled that most people will never see, but every reader will feel.

To the Employee Fanatix team: Hathaway Rabette, thank you for holding down the fort with the business when I needed to take deep dives to focus on finishing this book, and for always having my back. Ashley Rivera, thank you for always being honest and the person I can rely on to sniff test how aligned my thoughts are to my true self. Nikki Groom, thank you for supporting me in seeing this idea through in the expansion of my brand. I will always remember your great listening and empathy. Neil Hughes, you have been with me on my podcast journey since 2018, but we have been friends for many years before that. Thank you for giving me honest feedback, and for helping me re-brand the podcast, which allowed me to weave episode snippets into this book.

To my CMI Speaker Management team: thank you for helping me elevate my game and grow into the leader I am today. Your support, guidance, and belief in me have mattered more than I can fully express.

To my family: Luis, Gabriela, Sebastian, Dominic, and Matteo, thank you for supporting me, even when I seemed flustered and frustrated in the middle of this writing process. Thank you for giving me the space to write words that will help others, and for inspiring me to keep becoming better. Dominic, especially for the story in this book, thank you for serving as a mentor of mine and one of the steadiest leaders I know.

To others who have helped me on this journey: to my closest friends, Kimberly Davis (who always brings me back to center), Sara Ross (who kicks me in the butt and helps me realize the ways I might minimize myself and my thoughts and helps me expand my thinking), and Sylvie Di Giusto (who relates to me and also talks me off the cliff when I need it). Thank you for being the kind of friends who tell the truth with love. You have helped me see the error in my thinking at times, and you have made it easier for me to steady myself.

About the Author

Heather R. Younger, J.D., CSP, is a leadership and workplace culture keynote speaker, researcher, consultant, and four-time bestselling author whose work helps organizations build leaders and teams that can weather any storm.

Named an Inc. Top 50 Leadership and Management Expert and a Thinkers50 Radar Thought Leader, Heather brings more than 20 years of hands-on experience leading teams through high-stakes situations where results mattered, people depended on her, and decisions couldn't wait.

For years, she taught leaders how to care, how to listen, connect, and create workplaces where people feel valued. But at the pinnacle of her most successful year as an entrepreneur, she hit a wall. She realized she'd forgotten to include one person in all that care: herself.

That moment changed everything. She began to turn the mirror inward, to pause, listen to her own needs, and question what she valued and what she was sacrificing. What she discovered became the foundation of her signature C.A.R.E. framework for Unshakable Leadership™. When leaders are grounded and resourced in care, they become the calm in the chaos. And when leaders are unshakable, they create cultures where teams can breathe again.

Heather's research foundation includes analysis of more than 40,000 employee survey comments and 350+ leader interviews. This work grounds her keynotes, workshops, and consulting in what people actually experience at work; not just what looks good on paper.

She speaks to healthcare professionals, financial advisors, tech teams, and leaders across industries who show up with heart and purpose because they know their work matters and who are tired of being told to "be more resilient" without being given the tools to actually sustain themselves.

She is the author of four other books, *The Art of Caring Leadership*, *The Art of Self-Leadership*, *The Art of Active Listening*, and *The 7 Intuitive Laws of Employee Loyalty: Fascinating Truths About What It Takes to Create Truly Loyal and Engaged Employees*. She also hosts the podcast *Becoming Unshakable*, where she explores what it takes to lead with resilience, compassion, and purpose through candid conversations with executives, frontline leaders, and everyday changemakers.

Heather's clients span healthcare, financial services, technology, and beyond, including United Healthcare, Kaiser Permanente, the CDC, Prudential, DuPont, Stellantis, Con Edison, and Xerox. She partners with leaders who care deeply about the work they do and the people they serve and who are ready to stop pouring from an empty cup and start building something that lasts.

Index